The Complet

Discover Over 100 Recipes to Learn How to Cook Seafood and Fish Recipes and Weight Loss and Well-Being Journey

By

Lee A. Lesko

The trademarks that are used are without any consent, and the publication of the trademark is without permission or backing by the trademark owner. All trademarks and brands within this book are for clarifying purposes only and are the owned by the owners themselves, not affiliated with this document.

Table of contents

Introduction

In the current world, we as humans have become very conscious of our health. We mostly prefer organic diet over other artificially grown foods. Being on a diet has been the most popular answer we get whenever we ask someone about their health. It is a very famous saying that, "your health is directly proportional to your mood swings," if you eat healthy and eat right, you are always going to have a splendid and wonderful mood.

This book is a road map towards eating different and eating healthy. While, losing weight vegetarians feel the most difficulty as they lack the essential amino acid source in their diet. Pescatarians on the other hand are vegetarians but those who fill their essential protein source with the help of seafood in their diet.

In this book, you will learn everything about the Pescatarian diet, the history, and the origin of this diet. You will come across various benefits of adopting this dieting regime, and the overall effect of seafood on your health in the chapters of this book. There are also other dietetic plans that people adopt very often such as the Carnivore diet and the Vegetarian diet. You will learn the difference between all the three diets, and acquire the knowledge of the advantages, and disadvantages of all these diet plans.

Moving towards the main part of the book, the shopping list that you need to start your diet plan is also provided along with a sample meal plan that will assist you in making your own diet routine. Hundred recipes including breakfast, lunch, dinner, snacks, sweet dishes, and juices are mentioned in this cookbook that are very easy to make on your own in your kitchen.

So, why wait further when you can get healthy starting from today, let us dive into the pool of health together.

Chapter 1: Introduction to Pescatarian Diet

A Pescatarian is somebody who decides to eat a veggie diet; however who likewise eats fish, and other seafood products. It is a generally plant based eating regimen of whole grains, nuts, vegetables, whole produce, and solid fats, with fish assuming a key function as a principle protein source. Numerous Pescatarians likewise eat dairy and eggs.

Obviously, similarly as vegan diets can vary broadly, so can Pescatarian ones. It is conceivable to eat a meat free diet that is brimming with processed starches, junk food items and fish sticks, as opposed to a more advantageous one dependent on whole food sources.

1.1 History and Origins of Pescatarian Diet

The word vegetarian is defined by the Oxford Dictionary as 'a person who does not eat meat or fish, and sometimes other animal products, especially for moral, religious, or health reasons.' While this is a good broad definition of the vegetarian diet, the actual practice of vegetarianism is somewhat less clear cut.

There are several subcategories of vegetarianism including Ovolactarians, who eat dairy products, and eggs but abstain from meat, and Lactarians, who eat dairy products but abstain from meat and eggs. Some people include fish in their diet but still consider themselves vegetarians; a new name for this lifestyle, Pescatarian, has recently emerged.

Vegans are the strictest subcategory of the vegetarian movement, abstaining from all animal-based products. Strict followers of veganism do not eat honey, or wear leather, or wool. While religion sometimes calls for a vegetarian or vegan diet, over the years we have seen an increasing number of individuals choosing not to consume animal products based on their personal beliefs.

A portion of the principal self-announced Vegetarians were the Pythagoreans, a title got from the Greek logician Pythagoras, a founder of the mathematical Pythagorean hypothesis. In spite of the fact that Pythagoras lent his name to the meatless eating routine, it is muddled whether he followed a severe vegan routine or not. Some people speculate that along with a typical breakfast of nectar, and supper of grain bread with vegetables, he may have eaten fish also, which would have made him Pescatarian by the present principles.

Supporters of Pythagoras received his dietary limitations, accepting that they were useful in helping life span. The lessons of Pythagorus were first distributed in quite a while by Italian essayist, and Doctor Antonio Cocchi; in 1745 they were converted into English by Robert Dodsley. A record of his eating regimen additionally showed up in the Greek thinker Porphyry's book On Abstinence from Animal Food (third century). The compelling chronicled archive incorporates a portion of exactly the same contentions that cutting edge vegans use while lauding the benefits of a meatless eating regime. With vegetarianism on the rise, it is now common for restaurants to feature vegetarian menus, or meatless entrée alternatives. Grocery stores carry a large variety of vegetarian options, proving a strong market for meatless products. With proper attention to nutritional intake, it is entirely possible for vegetarians, and vegans to live a long and healthy life.

1.2 Benefits of Pescatarian Diet in terms of Nutrition

In the Pescatarian diet, a person's main source of animal protein comes from fish, and other seafood, such as shrimp etc. Eating a diet consisting mainly of plant-based foods has a variety of health benefits, which the addition of fish and fish products may enhance. However, some types of fish may absorb mercury from their environment, so certain people may need to limit their intake. Following are some benefits of the Pescatarian diet in terms of Nutrition:

1.   A Pescatarian diet may ensure individual's safety against colorectal diseases, or malignancies that influence the colon, and rectum. As indicated by a recent report, colorectal malignant growths are the subsequent driving reason for disease passing in the United States. The examination utilized information from a companion of more than 77,650 individuals, and found that the Pescatarian diet had a solid defensive impact against colorectal malignant growths.

2.   Following a plant-based eating routine can diminish the danger of type-2 diabetes, and metabolic disorder. Metabolic disorder incorporates conditions, for example, insulin opposition, hypertension, and heftiness. There is likewise proof that omega-3s present in greasy fish may diminish aggravation, however this proof originates from preliminaries of enhancements. Plant-based eating regimens are high in calming, and cell reinforcement operators, for example, flavonoids. Flavonoids have a scope of calming, and antidiabetic properties.

3.   Some people choose vegetarian diets because they disagree with factory farming practices, or killing animals for food. For people concerned about animal welfare, the Pescatarian diet may be a little more suitable. This is because some scientists argue that fish cannot feel pain.

4.   Eating fish, especially fatty fish, provides increased long-chain omega-3 fatty acid intake. An omega-3 fatty acid is an unsaturated fat that can be beneficial to people, and some omega-3s are integral for healthy living. People who eat fish have lower blood pressure, a lower risk of abnormal heart rhythms, and fewer fatal heart attacks than those who do not include fish in their diet.

5.   Plant-based diets can help a person maintain a healthy weight, and they also may help with weight loss when necessary. A Pescatarian diet may also be more healthful than some diets that rely on calorie deficits to reduce weight.

1.3 Effects of Seafood on Overall Health of an Individual

The foods we eat influence our health. Besides containing protein, and other nutrients such as vitamin D and selenium, fish (either finfish or shellfish) contain a specific type of fat, omega-3 fatty acids, that may reduce the risk of developing heart disease, and other medical problems.

Omega-3 fatty acids are found in fish especially oily fish such as salmon, sardines, and herring. These omega-3 fatty acids can help lower your blood pressure, lower your heart rate, and improve other cardiovascular risk factors. Eating fish reduces the risk of death from heart disease, the leading cause of death in both men, and women. Fish intake has also been linked to a lower risk of stroke, depression, and mental decline with age. For pregnant women, mothers who are breastfeeding, and women of childbearing age, fish intake is important because it supplies DHA, a specific omega-3 fatty acid that is beneficial for the brain development of infants.

Fishes help keep up cardiovascular wellbeing by assuming a function in the guideline of blood thickening, and vessel choking, and are significant for pre-birth and postnatal neurological turn of event. Fish may lessen tissue irritation, and ease the manifestations of rheumatoid joint pain, and may assume a valuable part in cardiovascular arrhythmia (unpredictable heartbeat), lessening sadness, and ending mental decrease in more established individuals.

Chapter 2: Comparison of Pescatarian Diet with Other Diets

Many healthy eaters are reducing their intake of meat, and other animal products to boost wellness. If you are considering different options, there are many different plant based eating plans to choose from. The Pescatarian diet is just one of them.

In this chapter you will see how the Pescatarian diet is different from the Vegetarian, and Carnivore diet.

2.1 Pescatarian Diet vs. Carnivore Diet

Being a Pescatarian is where you eat meat, but only meat that comes from the sea. Fish has a lot of iron in it, and that can benefit your health greatly. Plus, it is easier to be cruelty free when it comes to. A great way to become a Pescatarian is by finding a great local fish market near you. The biggest benefit includes the iron that fish have, the more fish you eat, the greater amount of iron you will have. Just as well, you will not be consuming land animals, so you will be more conscious when it comes to those types of meat. The downside is the price. Fish is more expensive, so you will have to work around that. Also, fish has a ton of mercury in it, so you will have to make sure to maintain that.

If you want to become more animal product conscious, but do not want to give up meat entirely, the carnivore diet is probably the way to go for you. You can do this by being aware of where your animal products are coming from. Happy farms are the best way to think about doing this.

An animal without a bunch of hormones injected in is going to be great for you. Furthermore, cage-free animals are happier. Animal cruelty free meat is a major thing.

Knowing where my meat is coming from makes you feel really good. Some farm animals do not ever see sunlight, let alone get to roam around.

Weight Loss

The Pescatarian diet may cause weight loss when portions are controlled while the Carnivore diet also cause the same effect of weight loss but unfortunately there is a drawback of not getting the proper nutrients the body needs that comes from plant based diets.

Health Risks

Carnivore diets come with nutritional deficiencies that can be a cause of big health risks for any individuals in the future. On the other hand one specific risk associated with a Pescatarian diet is the presence of mercury or heavy metals, a registered dietician. Fish, shellfish, and other seafood accumulate mercury in their bodies. As bigger fish eat smaller fish, this can drive up the concentration of these potentially dangerous toxins in the flesh of the larger fish.

Health Benefits

Carnivore, and Pescatarian both diets are very healthy for individuals, and they provide us a variety of nutrients that are unlikely to occur in the case of carnivore diets that lack plants on the whole and so lack all the nutrients that occur in plant based diets.

2.2 Pescatarian Diet vs. Vegetarian Diet

There are no exact rules that figure out what is a Pescatarian, and what is a Vegetarian. Furthermore, there are no guidelines that characterize how frequently you have to eat fish so as to be a Pescatarian. For instance, you might be a vegan who once in a while eats fish or you may remember it for each dinner. Nutritionists state that Pescatarians will in general be individuals who are wellbeing cognizant, and settle on careful decisions when arranging dinners. They might be people who are thinking about a vegan diet, and are utilizing a fish-based way to deal with plant-based eating. Or on the other hand they might be individuals who intend to follow a Pescatarian diet as long as possible, to dodge red meat.

Health Risks

One specific risk associated with a Pescatarian diet is the presence of mercury or heavy metals. Fish, shellfish, and other seafood accumulate mercury in their bodies. As bigger fish eat smaller fish, this can drive up the concentration of these potentially dangerous toxins in the flesh of the larger fish.

Overall Cost

Both Vegetarian and Pescatarian diets can be budget-friendly, especially if you are including conventionally grown products instead of seeking out only organic items. The addition of seafood in a Pescatarian diet could increase the cost, but choosing canned and frozen options, especially when they are on sale, can help reduce the cost. Red meat, and poultry can be expensive, so forgoing these purchases in favor of more fresh fruits and vegetables, whole grains, legumes and fish could reduce your overall shopping bill. As with any diet, the quality of the food is also important. Look for whole, unprocessed options rather than prepackaged or prepared foods. These whole foods that you cook yourself are usually less expensive than prepared foods.

Health Benefits

Both diets are considered majorly plant based. The people who are following these diets will achieve many of the benefits associated with plant based diets. This approach to eating when done right has been associated with plenty of health benefits including better control of blood pressure, better control of blood glucose, less inflammation, reduced cholesterol levels. These factors translate into improved heart health, a reduced risk of developing diabetes and a reduced risk of certain types of cancer.

Additionally Pescatarians have the added benefit of getting plenty of omega-3 fatty acids, which are known for their heart-protective and anti-inflammatory properties. Omega-3s are essential compounds that the body cannot make on its own. You have to ingest them as part of your diet or in supplement form. They are critical to maintaining cardiovascular health. Fatty fish, such as sardines, mackerel and salmon are rich sources of omega-3s.

Weight Loss

The Pescatarian diet may cause weight loss when portions are controlled while the Vegetarian diet also cause the same effect of weight loss if the portion size of the meals are quantified properly.

Chapter 3: Pescatarian Diet- Shopping List and Meal Plan

The Pescatarian diet originates from a Vegetarian diet, zeroing in on plant-based nourishments and fish, however dispensing with meat and poultry. Numerous individuals decided to turn into a Pescatarian on the grounds that it considers a smoother change to a plant-based eating routine and can be simpler to support in the drawn out when contrasted with a Vegetarian diet. In addition, fish is a finished wellspring of protein and has a large number of dietary advantages. Most Pescatarians like eggs and dairy for their eating routine, however some do not as this is an individual decision.

3.1 Grocery List- Foods You Need To Follow the Diet

Following is the grocery list that you need to follow before starting your Pescatarian diet:

- Beans and legumes
- All kinds of fish
- Tofu and tempeh
- Chia seeds
- All kinds of nuts
- Flax seeds
- Shellfish
- All kinds of fruits
- All kinds of vegetables
- Dairy products

- Eggs
- Brown rice
- Oatmeal
- Quinoa
- Different sauces: oyster sauce, chili sauce, soy sauce, Worcestershire sauce
- Whole wheat flour or bread
- Dried spices and mix herbs
- Different oils: canola oils, olive oil, sunflower oil

3.2 7 Day Sample Meal Plan of Pescatarian Diet

Day 1:

Breakfast: Scrambled eggs with cheese kcalories	125
Lunch: Lemon kale and salmon pasta kcalories	186
Snack: Green tea smoothie kcalories	183
Dinner: Buckwheat pasta salad kcalories	402
Total Calories kcalories	896

Day 2:

Breakfast: Egg muffin kcalories	105

Lunch: Caesar salad kcalories	186
Snack: Black current and kale smoothie kcalories	183
Dinner: Prawn Arabiata kcalories	434
Total Calories kcalories	908

Day 3:

Breakfast: Tomato Omlette kcalories	125
Lunch: Caribbean Salad with shrimp kcalories	192
Snack: Strawberry and cucumber juice kcalories	183
Dinner: Miso marinated cod with stir-fried greens kcalories	450
Total Calories kcalories	950

Day 4:

Breakfast: Date and Walnut Oatmeal kcalories	350
Lunch: Tofu and kale pesto sandwich kcalories	186

Snack: Green tea smoothie kcalories	183
Dinner: Prawn Arabiata kcalories	420
Total Calories kcalories	1139

Day 5:

Breakfast: Banana Egg pancakes kcalories	125
Lunch: Caesar salad kcalories	186
Snack: Mango and Pineapple smoothie kcalories	183
Dinner: Lemon kale salmon pasta kcalories	620
Total Calories kcalories	1122

Day 6:

Breakfast: Blueberry pancakes kcalories	509
Lunch: Potato soup kcalories	186
Snack: Green Juice kcalories	143

Dinner: New Orleans kcalories	416
Total Calories kcalories	1251

Day 7:

Breakfast: Oat and berry Acai bowl kcalories	501
Lunch: Shrimp Coronation salad kcalories	186
Snack: Melon and Grape Juice kcalories	125
Dinner: Baked salmon with mint dressing kcalories	350
Total Calories kcalories	1162

The above designed diet plans are made from the same recipes which are listed in the chapters below, and you can indulge variations into your meal plans according to your choices.

Chapter 4: Pescatarian Diet Recipes

The only thing worse than a bad meal is no meal at all. Luckily, that is not going to be an issue for you. Following are a lineup of some of the best Pescatarian meal ideas in this chapter. Each recipe is genuinely tasty, easy to make and nutritious.

4.1 Breakfast Recipes

1)   Caramelized Banana Dark Chocolate Oatmeal

Preparation time: 10 minutes

Cooking Time: 10 minutes

Serving: 1

Ingredients:

*   Olive oil spray

*   Water, one cup

*   Sliced medium banana, half

*   Dark chocolate chips, two tbsp.

*   Rolled oats, one cup

Instructions:

1.   In a small saucepan, bring water to a boil.

2.   Stir in oats and reduce heat to low.

3.   Simmer until oats have absorbed all of the liquid, three to five minutes.

4.　　While oats are cooking, spray a small non-stick skillet with olive oil.

5.　　Add sliced bananas in a single layer and cook over medium heat until caramelized, about three minutes per side.

6.　　Spoon oatmeal into a bowl and top with caramelized bananas, and chocolate chips.

2)　　Scrambled Eggs with Cheese

Preparation time: 5 minutes

Cooking Time: 12 minutes

Serving: 4-6

Ingredients:

- Mozzarella cheese, one cup
- Butter, three tbsp.
- Salt and Pepper, to taste
- Eggs, twelve

Instructions:

1.　　In a large nonstick pan with sloped sides, melt the butter over medium-low heat, being careful to not brown the butter.

2.　　If it begins to bubble, the heat is too high, so lower the heat to cook the eggs properly.

3.　　Meanwhile, in a large bowl, add the eggs and one teaspoon cold water.

4.　　Vigorously whisk until frothy and smooth.

5.　　Swirl the pan around to coat the butter on the bottom and up the sides.

6.   Pour the eggs into the pan and let sit for a few seconds.

7.   When the eggs begin to lightly set on the bottom, use the whisk to gently beat the eggs, and then allow them to sit for just a few seconds between beating them again.

8.   Curds will begin to form and increase throughout the cooking time. Repeat this process of whisking then resting the eggs for a few seconds until about 50 percent of the eggs are set and the rest are still wet.

9.   At this point, sprinkle the eggs with a pinch of salt and pepper and continue to whisk and rest alternately.

10.   Once the eggs are 75 percent done add the cheese and from this moment, continue to whisk the eggs until done. This entire process from pouring in the eggs to them being finished should take eight minutes.

11.   Remove from the heat and continue to scramble in the last seconds.

12.   Your dish is ready to be served.

3)   Breakfast Egg Muffins

Preparation time: 10 minutes

Cooking Time: 40 minutes

Serving: 12

Ingredients:

*   Yellow onion chopped, one

*   Turkey bacon, three slices

*   Cooking spray

- Salt and Pepper, to taste
- Eggs, six
- Chopped red bell pepper, one
- Shredded mozzarella cheese, half cup
- Chopped baby spinach, one cup
- Garlic powder, half tsp.
- Paprika, half tsp.
- Milk, three tbsp.

Instructions:

1. Preheat oven to 350° and grease a 12-cup muffin tin with avocado or coconut oil cooking spray or coconut oil.

2. In a large nonstick skillet over medium heat, cook turkey bacon until crispy, six and eight minutes.

3. Drain on a paper towel-lined plate, then crumble.

4. Add onion and bell pepper to skillet and cook until soft. Cook for approximately five minutes.

5. Add spinach and cook until wilted, two minutes more.

6. In a small bowl, whisk eggs, milk, paprika, and garlic powder and season with salt and pepper.

7. Fold in cooked vegetable mixture, turkey bacon, and mozzarella. Pour mixture into prepared muffin tin.

8. Bake until cooked through and golden for thirty minutes.

9. Your dish is ready to be served.

4) Chickpea Flour Pancakes

Preparation time: 5 minutes

Cooking Time: 5 minutes

Serving: 2

Ingredients:

- Water, one cup
- Olive oil, one tbsp.
- Cooking spray
- Salt and Pepper, to taste
- Chickpea flour, one cup
- Spring onions, one cup
- Chili flakes, half tsp.
- Turmeric, half tsp.
- Peas, half cup
- Chopped red bell peppers, half cup

Instructions:

1. Add the flour, water, turmeric, salt, pepper and chili flakes to a mixing bowl and give it a quick blend using a food processor or blender.

2. Leave it to settle for a few minutes while you heat up the oil or ghee in a non-stick pan.

3. The batter needs to look very runny.

4. Dice the veggies finely and add them to the mixture.

5. Use a tissue or similar to ensure the bottom of the pan is coated well in oil.

6.   Add about a ladle of the mixture and veggies when the pan is hot a medium heat should be just right.

7.   Cook for about three minutes the mixture will quickly start to firm.

8.   If you are using two pans, you can make two pancakes at the same time.

9.   Make sure you use a large pan here, you are aiming for thin pancakes.

10.   Use a large spatula to help you flip the pancakes, adding more oil underneath if necessary.

11.   Your pancakes are ready to serve.

5)   Dutch Banana Pancakes

Preparation time: 5 minutes

Cooking Time: 5 minutes

Serving: 2

Ingredients:
- Milk, half cup
- Flour, half cup
- Cooking spray
- Eggs, three
- Sugar, one tbsp.
- Nutmeg, half tsp.
- Butter, two tbsp.
- Sliced banana, one

Instructions:

1.	Mix all the ingredients together and make a smooth batter.

2.	Make sure you use a large pan here; you are aiming for perfect pancakes.

3.	Use a large spatula to help you flip the pancakes, adding more butter underneath if necessary.

4.	Your pancakes are ready to serve.

6)	Rubab Mango Oatmeal

Preparation time: 5 minutes

Cooking Time: 5 minutes

Serving: 1

Ingredients:
- Orange juice, half cup
- Oats, one cup
- Fresh rhubarb, one cup
- Milk, one and a half cup
- Salt, a pinch
- Brown sugar, three tbsp.
- Cinnamon, half tsp.
- Chopped pecans or any nuts, two tbsp.
- Chopped mango slices, one

Instructions:

1.   Combine milk, juice, oats, rhubarb, cinnamon and salt in a medium saucepan. Bring to a boil over medium-high heat.

2.   Reduce heat, cover and cook at a very gentle bubble, stirring frequently, until the oats and rhubarb are tender, about five minutes.

3.   Remove from the heat and let stand, covered, for five minutes.

4.   Stir in sweetener to taste.

5.   Garnish with nuts and mango slices.

7)   Easy Tomato Omelet

Preparation time: 5 minutes

Cooking Time: 5 minutes

Serving: 1

Ingredients:

*   Fresh basil, half cup
*   Spring onions, half cup
*   Cherry tomatoes, half cup
*   Eggs, two
*   Salt, a pinch
*   Red chili
*   Pepper, half tsp.

Instructions:

1.   Wash the tomatoes, chilies, and spring onion and chop into small pieces.

2.   Heat half the oil in a pan and fry the tomatoes for about two minutes.

3.   Set aside.

4.   Clean the pan with a tissue.

5.   Crack the eggs into a bowl and beat well with a fork, adding the salt and pepper

6.   Heat the rest of the oil in a pan on low to medium heat.

7.   Pour the egg mix into the pan.

8.   Using a spatula, ruffle the omelet so it does not stick.

9.   As you create gaps tilt the pan so the liquid fills the spaces.

10.   Let it cook for about two minutes and when the egg mixture looks nearly cooked drop on the tomatoes and basil.

11.   Fold the empty half of the omelet on top of the other.

12.   Slide it onto a plate the heat from closing the omelet will finish cooking the inside.

13.   Your dish is ready to be served.

8)   Breakfast Burrito

Preparation time: 15 minutes

Cooking Time: 15 minutes

Serving: 4

Ingredients:

* Wheat tortillas, four
* Chopped red onions, half cup
* Red bell pepper, half cup
* Black beans, one cup
* Eggs, four
* Hot sauce
* Salt, a pinch
* Canola oil, one tbsp.
* Red chili, one tbsp.
* Pepper, half tsp.
* Sour cream, half cup
* Shredded mozzarella cheese, one cup
* Chopped tomato, half cup
* Chopped avocado, half cup

Instructions:

1.   Heat the canola oil in a large nonstick skillet over a medium-high heat.

2.   Cook the onions and peppers until onions are softened and peppers are slightly charred, about eight minutes.

3.   Add black beans and red pepper flakes and cook until warmed through, another three minutes.

4.   Season with salt and pepper and transfer to a dish.

5.   Whisk together the eggs and egg whites then stir in the cheese.

6.   Spray the skillet with cooking spray, and reheat the skillet over a medium heat. Reduce heat to low and add eggs, scrambling until cooked through, about three minutes.

7.   Spread each tortilla with one tablespoon each sour cream and salsa, then layer with some of the black bean mixture, some of the scrambled eggs, some diced tomato and some of the avocado.

8.   Season, to taste, with hot sauce.

9.   Roll up burrito-style and serve hot.

9)   The Runner's Sandwich

Preparation time: 5 minutes

Cooking Time: 5 minutes

Serving: 1

Ingredients:

- Bread, four slices

- Olives, half cup

- Sun dried tomatoes, half cup

- Capers, two tbsp.

- Fresh basil, half cup

- Salt, a pinch

- Canola oil, one tbsp.

- Red chili, one tbsp.

- Pepper, half tsp.

- Oregano, half tsp.

- Shredded mozzarella cheese, one cup

Instructions:

1. Roughly chop the cheese, tomatoes, olives and capers and throw into a mixing bowl.

2. Add the herbs, salt and pepper.

3. Use a fork to mix up and mash the ingredients a little not too much.

4. If you are using very soft bread then pop it in the toaster or pan without oil for a minute or so not to toast it, just to harden the outside.

5. If the bread is already a hard type.

6. Spread the mix on the bottom slices; add the other slices on top.

7. Squish down.

8. Heat the pan and put the sandwich in.

9. Put a lid on the pan.

10. Cook for three to four minutes, squishing down with a spatula occasionally, then flip and cook the other side the same way.

11. Both outsides should be nice and crispy, the insides melting together.

12.   Your sandwich is ready to be served.

10)   Banana Egg Pancakes

Preparation time: 5 minutes

Cooking Time: 10 minutes

Serving: 6

Ingredients:

- Baking powder, two tsp.
- Coconut flour powder six tbsp.
- Ripe banana, two
- Vanilla extracts, one tsp.
- Eggs, two
- Oil
- Maple syrup
- Fresh berries
- Coconut yogurt
- Seeds
- Nut butter

Instructions:

1.   To a large mixing bowl, add bananas and mash until only small bits remain.

2.   Then add baking powder and vanilla extract and use a fork or whisk to mash until thoroughly combined.

3.   Next add eggs, break yolks with a fork or whisk, and whisk thoroughly until well combined.

4.   Lastly, add coconut flour one tbsp. at a time until a thick but scoopable batter is achieved.

5.   If you add too much coconut flour, add a little dairy free milk to thin.

6.   Heat a large skillet over medium heat.

7.   Once hot, add a little cooking oil to coat the pan.

8.   Then spoon in roughly three tbsp. amounts of batter and reduce heat to low. These benefit from cooking slower and lower than your average pancakes. Cover with a lid to help the center cook through.

9.   Cook for three to four minutes, then remove lid and flip carefully.

10.   Transfer cooked pancakes to the preheated oven on the prepared baking sheet.

11.   To serve, top with desired toppings, such as nut butter, sliced bananas or fresh fruit, dairy-free yogurt, or maple syrup.

11)   Coffee Chia Pudding

Preparation time: 5 minutes

Cooking Time: 10 minutes

Serving: 2

Ingredients:

*   Almond milk, one cup

- Vanilla extract, one tsp.
- Maple syrup, one tbsp.
- Whipped cream
- Coffee, powder, one tbsp.
- Chia seeds, half cup

Instructions:

1.   Combine all the things together except the whipped cream.

2.   Serve them in a bowl and top with whipped cream.

3.   Your dish is ready to be served.

12)   Eggs in a Cloud

Preparation time: 10 minutes

Cooking Time: 10 minutes

Serving: 2

Ingredients:
- Salt, one pinch
- Mixed cheese, half cup
- Eggs, two

Instructions:

1.   Preheat the oven to 450 degrees with a rack in the middle.

2.	Line a roasting pan, or baking sheet that can take high temperatures without warping, with parchment paper.

3.	Separate the egg yolks from the whites.

4.	Make sure there are no little pieces of egg yolk in the whites or you will have difficulty getting the whites to beat properly.

5.	It helps if you are making more than one egg nest to keep each egg yolk in a separate prep bowl.

6.	Place the egg whites in a very clean mixer bowl.

7.	Add a small pinch of salt to the egg whites.

8.	Beat the egg whites with a whisk attachment in a mixer, starting on low speed and then slowly increasing to high speed, until stiff peaks form.

9.	Your dish is ready to be served.

13)	Buttermilk Pancakes

Preparation time: 10 minutes

Cooking Time: 10 minutes

Serving: 4

Ingredients:

• 	Salt, one pinch

• 	All-purpose flour, two cup

• 	Eggs, two

• 	Unsalted butter, three tbsp.

• 	Sugar three tbsp.

- Baking powder, one tsp.

- Baking soda, one tsp.

- Buttermilk, two cups

- Canola oil, for cooking

Instructions:

1.   Heat the oven to 325 degrees.

2.   Whisk flour, sugar, baking powder, baking soda and kosher salt together in a bowl.

3.   Using the whisk, make a well in the center.

4.   Pour the buttermilk into the well and crack eggs into buttermilk.

5.   Pour the melted butter into the mixture.

6.   Starting in the center, whisk everything together, moving towards the outside of the bowl, until all ingredients are incorporated.

7.   Heat a large nonstick griddle or skillet, preferably cast-iron, over low heat for about five minutes.

8.   Add one tablespoon oil to the skillet.

9.   Turn heat up to medium low and using a measuring cup, ladle the batter into the skillet.

10.   Flip pancakes after bubbles rise to surface and bottoms brown, about two minutes. Cook until the other sides are lightly browned.

11.   Remove pancakes to a wire rack set inside a rimmed baking sheet, and keep in heated oven until all the batter is cooked and you are ready to serve.

14) Baked Eggs with Spinach and Tomatoes

Preparation time: 10 minutes

Cooking Time: 10 minutes

Serving: 4

Ingredients:

- Salt, one pinch
- Eggs, four
- Chili flakes, three tbsp.
- Butter, one tsp.
- Chopped tomatoes, two cups
- Spinach, one cup

Instructions:

1. Heat oven to 200 degrees.

2. Put the spinach into a colander, and then pour over a kettle of boiling water to wilt the leaves.

3. Squeeze out excess water and divide between four small ovenproof dishes.

4. Mix the tomatoes with the chili flakes and some seasoning, then add spinach while shifting the material in dishes.

5. Make a small well in the center of each and crack in an egg.

6. Bake for ten mins or more depending on how you like your eggs.

7.   Serve with crusty bread.

15)   Almond and Cherry Oatmeal

Preparation time: 5 minutes

Cooking Time: 5 minutes

Serving: 4

Ingredients:
- Dried oats, half cup
- Vanilla almond milk, three cups
- Salt, a pinch
- Cherries, one cup

Instructions:

1.   Stir together oats, almond milk, and salt in a large microwave safe bowl.

2.   Microwave on high for five minutes, stirring every two minutes, until oats are soft and most of the liquid has been absorbed.

3.   Stir in cherries.

4.   Spoon into bowls and serve while hot.

16)   Fluffy Quinoa Egg Muffin

Preparation time: 10 minutes

Cooking Time: 40 minutes

Serving: 12

Ingredients:

- Yellow onion chopped, one
- Quinoa, half cup
- Cooking spray
- Salt and Pepper, to taste
- Eggs, six
- Chopped red bell pepper, one
- Shredded mozzarella cheese, half cup
- Chopped baby spinach, one cup
- Garlic powder, half tsp.
- Paprika, half tsp.
- Milk, three tbsp.

Instructions:

1. Preheat oven to 350° and grease a 12-cup muffin tin with avocado or coconut oil cooking spray or coconut oil.

2. In a large nonstick skillet over medium heat, cook quinoa for six and eight minutes.

3. Drain on a paper towel-lined plate, then crumble.

4. Add onion and bell pepper to skillet and cook until soft approximately five minutes.

5. Add spinach and cook until wilted, two minutes more.

6. In a small bowl, whisk eggs, milk, paprika, and garlic powder and season with salt and pepper.

7.   Fold in cooked vegetable mixture, quinoa, and mozzarella. Pour mixture into prepared muffin tin.

8.   Bake until cooked through and golden for thirty minutes.

9.   Your dish is ready to be served.

17)   Mushroom Scrambled Egg

Serving: 1

Preparation time: 5 minutes

Cook time: 5 minutes

Ingredients:

- 25g kale, chopped
- 1 tsp ground turmeric
- One egg
- 5g parsley finely chopped
- 1 tsp mild curry powder
- ½ sliced bird's eye chili
- sliced button mushrooms
- 1 tsp extra virgin olive oil

Instructions:

1.   Make a paste of curry powder and turmeric by adding little water

2.   Lightly warm the kale by steaming for 2 minutes

3.   Fry the mushroom and bird's eye chili in a frying pan till they turn brown and soften on medium heat.

4.   Now add spice paste and egg, cook on medium heat.

5.   Add kale and cook on medium heat for one more minute.

6.   Add parsley and mix it

7.   It is ready to serve.

18)   Smoked Salmon Omelet

Serving: 1

Preparation time: 5 minutes

Cooking time: 4 minutes

Total time: 9 minutes

Ingredients:
- 100 g Smoked salmon, cut
- One tsp. extra virgin olive oil
- 2 Medium eggs
- 10 g chopped arugula leaves
- 1/2 tsp. capers
- One tsp. chopped parsley

Instructions:

1.   Break the eggs into a bowl and whisk well. Include the salmon, tricks, rocket, and parsley.

2.   Warm the olive oil in a non-stick skillet until hot yet not smoking. Include the egg blend and, utilizing a spatula or fish cut, move the blend around the container until it is even.

3.   Decrease the heat on the stove and let the omelet cook through.

4.   Slide the spatula around the edges and move up or overlay the omelet fifty-fifty to serve.

5.   It is ready to serve.

19)   Shakshuka

Serving: 6

Preparation time: 15 minutes

Cook time: 20 minutes

Total Time: 35 minutes

Ingredients:

•   One substantial red ringer pepper or broiled red chime pepper

•   One huge onion, diced

•   ¼ teaspoon fine ocean salt

•   Two cloves garlic, squeezed or minced

•   Six enormous eggs

•   Two tablespoons tomato puree

•   One to two tablespoons olive oil

•   One teaspoon ground cumin

•   ½ teaspoon smoked paprika

- ¼ teaspoon red pepper drops, decrease or overlook if touchy to flavor

- One enormous can squashed tomatoes, ideally fire-broiled

- ½ cup disintegrated feta

- Two tablespoons slashed new cilantro or level leaf parsley, and cilantro or parsley leaves for embellishing

- Newly ground dark pepper, to taste

- Dry bread or pita, for serving

Instructions:

1. Preheat the stove to 375 degrees Fahrenheit. Warm the oil in an enormous, broiler safe pan over the medium stove.

2. Once gleaming, add in the onion, ringer pepper, and salt. Cook, regularly mixing, until the onions are delicate and turning translucent, around four to six minutes.

3. Include the garlic, tomato puree, cumin, paprika, and red pepper pieces. Cook, blending continually, until quite fragrant, one to two minutes.

4. Pour in the squashed tomatoes with their juices and include the cilantro. Mix, and let the blend go to a stew. Diminish the stove heat as important to keep up a delicate stew, and cook for 5 minutes to give the flavors time to merge.

5. Switch off the stove. Taste it, and include salt and pepper as preferred. Utilize the rear of a spoon to make a well close to the border and split the egg legitimately into it. Delicately spoon a touch of the tomato blend over the whites to help contain the egg.

6. Rehash with the staying 4 to 5 eggs, contingent upon what number of you can fit. Sprinkle somewhat salt and pepper over the eggs.

7. Cautiously move the pan to the broiler and heat for 8 to 12 minutes, frequently checking once you arrive at 8 minutes. They're done when the egg whites are an obscure white, and the yolks have risen a piece however are still delicate. They should, at present, wiggle in the focuses when you shimmy the container.

8. Utilizing broiler gloves move the hot pan to a safe warmth surface like an oven. Top with the disintegrated feta, new cilantro leaves, and increasingly red pepper drops. However, you may prefer it. Serve in bowls with dry bread.

9. It is ready to serve.

20) Blueberry Pancakes

Serving: 12

Preparation time: 10 minutes

Cook time: 10 minutes

Total time: 20 minutes

Ingredients:
- One egg
- One cup flour
- 3/4 cup milk
- Two tablespoons softened spread
- Two tablespoons white vinegar

- Two tablespoons sugar
- 1/2 teaspoon baking soda
- One teaspoon baking powder
- 1/2 teaspoon salt
- One cup blueberries
- more margarine for the container

Instructions:

1. Blend the milk and vinegar and let it sit for a moment or two.

2. Whisk the dry things together. Whisk the egg, milk, and softened spread into the dry ones until simply consolidated.

3. Heat a non-stick pan over a medium stove. Dissolve a little smear of margarine in the pan.

4. Pour around 1/3 cup of the mixture into the hot pan and spread it level like it will be entirely thick. Throw a couple of blueberries on top. Cook until you see little air pockets on top and the edges beginning to solidify. Flip and cook for another one to two minutes until they cooked through.

5. Present with margarine and maple syrup.

6. It is ready to eat.

21) Black Bean Scrambled Eggs

Serving: 1

Preparation time: 10 minutes

Cook time: 15 minutes

Total time: 25 minutes

Ingredients:

- 1/3 medium avocado

- Two huge egg whites

- 1/2 tsp. olive oil

- One tbsp. salsa, no sugar included 1/2 cup dark beans, no sugar included whenever canned

- 1/4 medium onion, diced red onion is the most delicious

Instructions:

1.   Sauté your onions in the oil in a non-stick pan.

2.   Include your eggs and scramble or cook.

3.   When eggs are close to cooked, mix in your beans and cook sufficiently long to warm them up.

4.   Move to a plate and top with salsa and avocado.

5.   It is ready to serve.

22)   Strawberry Chocolate chips and Buckwheat Pancakes

Serving: 2

Preparation time: 5 minutes

Cook time: 30 minutes

Total time: 35 minutes

Ingredients:

- One huge egg
- One cup buckwheat flour
- One teaspoon baking powder
- Two tablespoons coconut sugar
- One tablespoon vanilla concentrate
- Two tablespoons additional virgin olive oil
- One teaspoon ground cinnamon
- 1/4 teaspoon fit salt
- 3/4 cup unsweetened cashew milk (or sans dairy milk of your decision)
- 1/2 cup hacked strawberries
- 1/4 cup dull chocolate chips
- Discretionary toppings:
- Ground flax seeds
- Maple syrup
- Chocolate Chips
- Diced Strawberries

Instructions:

1.   Gently oil a pan and pre-heat on the medium stove.

2.   In a medium-sized bowl, whisk together the flour, sugar, heating powder, cinnamon, and salt.

3.   In a little bowl, whisk together the milk, oil, vanilla, and egg. Add the wet blend to the dry blend and mix until simply joined. Do not over blend. Overlay in the strawberries and chocolate chips.

4.   Scoop out around 1/2 cup of the prepared mixture into the warmed skillet and spread it out into a 5-inch circle.

5.   Cook for 4-5 minutes, or until the edges begin to cook and a couple of air pockets show up on top. Flip and cook for another 2-3 minutes.

6.   Present with maple syrup and preferred garnishes.

7.   It is ready to serve.

23)   Herb Omelet with Fita and Beans:

Serving: 2

Preparation time: 10 minutes

Cook time: 10 minutes

Total time: 20 minutes

Ingredients:

*   200g wide beans, podded weight

*   Two little cubes of unsalted margarine

*   Four medium eggs

*   75g vegan feta cheddar disintegrated or crumbled

*   1/2 pack tarragon leaves as it were

*   1/2 pack chives

*   1/2 pack level leaf parsley leaves as it were

*   1/2 lemon zest

Instructions:

1. Heat a pan of water to bubble and whiten the expansive beans for two minutes until simply delicate.

2. Deplete and revive under normal temperature running water.

3. Evacuate the external skin of the bean, to uncover the brilliant internal parts.

4. Split the eggs into a bowl and beat with a fork. Finely slash the herbs and speed into the eggs, alongside the vast majority of the lemon get-up-and-go and a lot of salt and newly ground dark pepper.

5. Warm a non-stick skillet over a medium-high stove. Include a little cube of spread at that point, while frothing, include in a large portion of the egg blend.

6. Utilize a spatula to move the egg around the container, letting it flood the spaces until it is nearly cooked.

7. Disperse a large portion of the cheddar and a large portion of the beans over the omelet.

8. Leave for 20-30 seconds, so the underside is completely set, and an exquisite brilliant earthy colored at that point overlay down the middle and slide onto a plate. Rehash for a subsequent omelet and serve quickly, dispersed with the held zest of lemon.

9. It is ready to serve.

24) Date and Walnut Oatmeal

Serving: 1

Preparation time: 5 minutes

Cook time: 7 minutes

Total time: 12 minutes

Ingredients:

- 1/2 cups water
- 1/2 tsp. salt (discretionary)
- Two cups of oats
- 2/3 cup cleaved walnuts
- 2/3 cup cleaved dates

Instructions:

1.   Heat the water and salt to the point of boiling.

2.   Mix in the oats, walnuts, and dates.

3.   Slow down the stove to medium.

4.   Spread and cook for five minutes, mixing on more than one occasion.

5.   Switch off the stove and let it cool down for two to three minutes before serving.

6.   Present it with a sprinkle of earthy colored sugar or turbinado sugar and a sprinkle of milk or creamer.

7.   Sprinkle over extra dates and walnuts whenever wanted.

8.   It is ready to eat.

25)   Buckwheat Porridge

Serving: 2

Preparation time: 6 minutes

Cook time: 12 minutes

Total time: 18 minutes

Ingredients:

- Two cups of warm water
- One cup buckwheat, rinsed

Instructions:

1.   Add buckwheat groats and water to a little pot to a medium high warmth. Heat to the point of boiling. Spread the pot with a top and put heat on low. Stew ten minutes, don't overcook. You can utilize a clock.

2.   Following ten minutes, turn off warmth. Try not to open the cover, permit it to steam for an additional five minutes.

3.   Cushion with a fork and serve. Top with fruits, almond milk, and a sprinkle of vanilla, a scramble of cinnamon, and a shower of maple syrup or nectar.

4.   It is ready to serve.

4.2 Lunch Recipes

26)   Tangy Veggie Wrap

Preparation time: 6 minutes

Cook time: 12 minutes

Serving: 2

Ingredients:

- Sunflower seeds three tbsp.

- Carrots, two small

- Ginger one thumb

- Bell pepper half

- Red onion one

- Cottage cheese, half cup

- Sour cream, two tbsp.

- Lemon zest, one tsp.

- Mustard, three tsp.

- Wraps, two

- Spinach, half cup

- Salt and pepper to taste

- Bean sprouts, half cup

Instructions:

1.   Roast the sunflower seeds in a pan without any oil until golden brown.

2.   Peel and grate the carrots. Wash and dice the bell pepper.

3.   Peel the onion and cut in thin rings.

4.   Wash and drain the spinach.

5.   Wash the bean sprouts with cold water and let them dry.

6.   Peel the ginger and grate it into a bowl.

7.   Add the cottage cheese, sour cream, lemon zest and mustard, and mix it well.

8.   Spread the dressing mixture onto the wraps.

9.   Lay out the spinach leaves on top.

10.   Put the carrots, bell pepper, onions and bean sprouts in a wide line down the middle and sprinkle the roasted sunflower seeds on top.

11.   Season with a dash of salt and pepper and fold the wraps a little on both sides, then at the bottom and roll it as tightly as possible.

12.   Cut the wraps into halves and serve.

27)   King Prawn Stir Fry with Buckwheat Noodles

Serving: 1

Preparation time: 10 minutes

Cook time: 10 minutes

Total time: 20 minutes

Ingredients:

*   150 g shelled crude lord prawns, deveined

*   Two tbsp. tamari

*   Two tbsp. additional virgin olive oil

*   75 g soba (buckwheat) noodles

*   One garlic clove, finely hacked

*   One 10,000 foot bean stew, finely hacked

*   One tsp. ginger, finely hacked

*   20 g red onion, cut

*   40 g celery

*   75 g green beans, diced

- Kale 50g, generally diced
- 100g chicken stock
- 5g lovage or celery leaves

Instructions:

1. Heat a skillet over a high stove, at that point, cook the prawns in one teaspoon of the tamari and one teaspoon of the oil for two to three minutes.

2. Move the prawns to a plate. Wipe the work out with kitchen paper, as you're going to utilize it once more.

3. Cook the noodles in bubbling water for five to eight minutes or as instructed on the bundle. Channel and put in a safe spot.

4. In the meantime, fry the garlic, stew and ginger, red onion, celery, beans, and kale in the rest of the oil over a medium-high warmth for two to three minutes.

5. Add the stock and bring to the bubble, at that point stew for a moment or two, until the vegetables are cooked yet crunchy.

6. Include the prawns, noodles, and lovage or celery leaves to the container, mix it thoroughly, and remove from the stove. It is ready to be eaten.

28) Lemon Kale Salmon Pasta

Serving: 2

Nutritional Value: 620 calories

Preparation time: 10 minutes

Cook time: 15 minutes

Total time: 25 minutes

Ingredients:

- 4 oz wheat spaghetti (115 g)
- One boneless, skinless salmon, cubed
- Five tablespoons additional virgin olive oil
- Two cloves garlic, minced
- ¼ teaspoon red pepper chips
- 2 cups wavy kale (135 g), remove the ribs
- One lemon
- One tablespoon lemon juice
- legitimate salt, to taste
- ground dark pepper, to taste

Instructions:

1. Bubble salted water and cook the pasta for one moment, not exactly the time showed on the bundle. At the point when the pasta is done cooking, save ¼ cup (60 ml) of pasta water.

2. In the interim, heat two tablespoons of olive oil in a cast-iron skillet. Season cubed salmon with salt and pepper, add it to the skillet, and earthy colored it on each side. When cooked thoroughly around two to four minutes, remove from skillet and hold.

3. Cook three tablespoons of olive oil in a skillet and include garlic and red pepper drops. Cook until fragrant, around one minute.

4.   Include kale, zests of lemon, lemon juice, salt, and saved pasta water. Cook until kale is delicate, around three minutes.

5.   Include cooked salmon and pasta. Mix to cover and serve right away.

29)   Pot Prawns and Kale Curry

Serving: 4

Preparation time: 8 minutes

Cook time: 2 minutes

Total time: 10 minutes

Ingredients:

- Two cups chopped onions

- Two garlic cloves, minced or grated

- 1/2 inch ginger, minced or grated

- Two medium roman tomatoes, chopped, about 1 cup

- Four teaspoons coriander powder

- 1/2 to 1 teaspoon cayenne pepper powder, depending on your spice level

- 1/2 teaspoon turmeric powder

- One cinnamon stick

- Two cardamoms

- Two cloves

- 1/4 teaspoon fennel seeds

- Prawns, one pound

- Four stalks kale, ribs removed and coarsely chopped
- 1/2 cup coconut milk
- One cup of water
- 11/2 to 2 teaspoons salt, divided (or as per your taste)

Instructions:

1. Set your Pot to sauté, include vegetable oil when hot. Include every entire flavor and let toast for a few moments.

2. Include all spices, sauté until onions turn translucent, around four minutes.

3. Sauté until tomatoes are soft, flavors are toasted well, and it starts to turn gleaming. Ensure you sauté like clockwork at this stage, causing sure that it doesn't to consume at the base.

4. Set manual for five minutes, ensuring the valve is set at fixing position.

5. Following five minutes, let your pot be in warm mode for two to four minutes. Go valve to vent and discharge the pressure.

6. Check for salt and present with your preferred side dish or cool and pack into boxes for use afterwards.

30)   Baked Tofu Wraps

Serving: 6

Nutritional Value: 360 calories

Preparation time: 15 minutes

Cook time: 30 minutes

Total time: 45 minutes

Ingredients:

- One square of extra-firm tofu depleted and squeezed.
- Six tablespoons corn-starch
- ⅓ cup unsweetened almond milk or milk of decision
- One cup oats
- Two tablespoon olive or avocado oil
- ½ teaspoon paprika
- One teaspoon dried oregano
- ½ teaspoon salt
- ¼ teaspoon dark pepper
- Six entire wheat wraps or tortillas
- Discretionary sauces and toppings
- 5g lovage or celery leaves

Instructions:

1.   Preheat broiler to 425 Fahrenheit and line an enormous preparing sheet with material paper. Put in a safe spot.

2.　　　Cut squeezed tofu into 24 little square shapes (does not need to be definite, fundamentally simply make them reduced down). Spot tofu shapes in a bowl.

3.　　　Next, join in the oats, oil, paprika, oregano, salt, and pepper in a shallow bowl until all around consolidated.

4.　　　Set up your tofu toward the start, trailed by corn starch in a shallow bowl, at that point a bowl of almond milk, lastly a shallow bowl with the breadcrumb blend. Toward the stopping point ought to be the material lined preparing sheet.

5.　　　Coat tofu pieces by dunking each piece into the corn starch, at that point the almond milk, and afterward the breadcrumb blend (once more, make a point to cover all the sides). Spot covered tofu on the readied heating sheet and rehash with extra tofu. Make sure to keep covered tofu pieces at any rate one to two inches separated on the preparing sheet.

6.　　　Prepare tofu for twenty five minutes, flip, and cook another five to ten minutes.

7.　　　Remove from the stove. Alternatively, you can hurl your tofu in BBQ sauce, and afterward gather your wraps.

8.　　　They are ready to eat.

31)   Tofu and Kale Pesto Sandwich

Serving: 2

Preparation time: 15 minutes

Cook time: 5 minutes

Total time: 20 minutes

Ingredients:

- Smoked tofu, seven ounce
- Olive oil, 5-6 tbsp.
- Walnuts, half cup
- Yeast, one tsp.
- Italian herb mix, two tsp.
- Kale, one cup
- Minced garlic, one
- ½ teaspoon salt
- ¼ teaspoon dark pepper
- Zucchini, one
- Carrot, one
- Wheat buns, two
- Lettuce

Instructions:

1.   First make the kale pesto.

2.   Put all ingredients into a blender or food processor and blend until smooth.

3.   Cut the tofu into thin strips.

4.   In a medium pan, heat some olive oil and stir-fry the tofu for about two minutes on each side until it is brown and crispy.

5.   If you want you can also add about half a teaspoon of soy sauce. Once the tofu is done, put it aside.

6.   Heat some more olive oil and cook the zucchini slices for another three minutes. Season with salt, pepper, and Italian spices (such as oregano, basil, rosemary, thyme).

7.   Cut the sandwiches in half and generously coat both sides with kale pesto.

8.   Add the lettuce, the tofu, the carrots, and the grilled zucchini.

32)   Sautéed Kale

Serving: 4

Nutritional Value: 98 calories

Preparation time: 5 minutes

Cook time: 20 minutes

Total time: 25 minutes

Ingredients:

•   One tablespoon in addition to one teaspoon extra-virgin olive oil for later use

•   1/2 pounds kale, ribs evacuated, coarsely cleaved

•   ½ cup of water

•   Two cloves garlic, minced

- ¼ teaspoon squashed red pepper

- Two to three teaspoons sherry vinegar or red-wine vinegar

- ¼ teaspoon salt

Instructions:

1. Warm one tablespoon oil in a broiler over a medium stove.

2. Include kale and cook, hurling with two huge spoons, until brilliant green, around one moment.

3. Include water; lessen warmth to medium-low, spread and cook, mixing at times, until the kale is delicate, about fifteen minutes.

4. Push kale aside, include the staying one teaspoon oil to the unfilled side and cooking garlic, and squash red pepper in it until it is fragrant, Switch off from the stove and hurl together. Mix in vinegar to taste and salt.

5. It is ready to serve.

33) Shrimp Butternut Squash and Date Tagine

Serving: 4

Nutritional Value: 244 calories

Preparation time: 15 minutes

Cook time: 1 hour and 15 minutes

Total time: 1 hour and 30 minutes

Ingredients:

- Two tablespoons olive oil

- One red onion, cut

- 2cm ginger, ground

- Two garlic cloves, ground or squashed

- One teaspoon bean stew drops (or to taste)

- Two teaspoons cumin seeds

- One cinnamon stick

- Two teaspoons ground turmeric

- 800g Shrimps

- ½ teaspoon salt

- 100g Medjool dates, hollowed and slashed

- 400g tin slashed tomatoes, in addition to a large portion of a jar of water

- 500g butternut squash cut into 1cm shapes

- 400g tin chickpeas, depleted

- Two tablespoons new coriander (in addition to this extra for decorations in the end)

- Buckwheat, couscous, flatbreads or rice to serve

Instructions:

1.   Preheat your broiler to 140 Celsius.

2.   Drizzle around two tablespoons of olive oil into an enormous ovenproof pot or cast iron goulash dish. Add in the previously diced onion and cook on a delicate heat, with the cover on, for around 5 minutes, until the onions are mellowed yet not earthy colored.

3. Add the ground garlic and ginger, bean stew, cumin, cinnamon, and turmeric. Mix well and cook for progressively one minute with the top off. Include a sprinkle of water in the event that it gets excessively dry.

4. Next include the shrimps. Mix well to cover the meat in the onions and flavors and afterward include the salt, slashed dates, and tomatoes, in addition to about a large portion of a container of water (100-200ml).

5. Bring the tagine to bubble and afterward put the top on and put in your preheated broiler for 1 hour and 15 minutes.

6. Thirty minutes before the finishing of the cooking time, include the cleaved butternut squash and chickpeas. Mix everything together, set the top back on, and come back to the broiler for the last 30 minutes of cooking.

7. When the tagine is prepared, quickly remove from the stove and mix through the cleaved coriander. Present with buckwheat, couscous, flatbreads, or basmati rice.

8. It is ready to be served.

34) Prawn Arabiata

Serving: 1

Nutritional Value: 420 calories

Preparation time: 40 minutes

Cook time: 30 minutes

Total time: 1 hour and 10 minutes

Ingredients:

• 125-150 g Raw or cooked prawns

- 65 g Buckwheat pasta
- One tbsp Extra virgin olive oil

For the sauce:

- One tsp Dried blended herbs
- 40 g Red onion, finely cleaved
- 30 g Celery, finely cleaved
- One Bird's eye bean stew, finely cleaved
- One tsp Extra virgin olive oil
- One Garlic clove, finely cleaved
- One tbsp Chopped parsley
- Two tbsp White wine (discretionary)
- 400 g Tinned cleaved tomatoes

Instructions:

1.   Fry the onion, garlic, celery, and bean stew and dried herbs in the oil over a medium-low stove for one to two minutes.

2.   Turn the warmth up to medium, include the wine, and cook for one moment. Include the tomatoes and leave the sauce to stew over medium-low heat for 20–30 minutes, until it has a decent creamy consistency.

3.   If you feel the sauce is getting too thick, essentially include a little water.

4.   While the sauce is cooking, Take a skillet of water and boil it till bubbles appear and cook the pasta as indicated on the parcel.

5.   At the point when prepared exactly as you would prefer, channel, hurl with the olive oil and keep in the skillet until required.

6.   If you are utilizing crude prawns, add them to the sauce and cook for a further three to four minutes until they have turned pink and murky, include the parsley and serve.

7.   In the event that you are utilizing cooked prawns, include them with the parsley, boil the sauce till bubbles appear and serve.

8.   Add the cooked pasta to the sauce, blend completely yet tenderly and serve.

35)   Baked Turmeric Salmon

Serving: 1

Nutritional Value: 358 calories

Preparation time: 15 minutes

Cook time: 10 minutes

Total time: 25 minutes

Ingredients:

• 125-150 g Skinned Salmon

• 1 tsp Extra virgin olive oil

• 1 tsp ground turmeric

• 1/4 Juice of a lemon

For celery:

• 1 tsp Extra virgin olive oil

• 40 g Red onion, finely diced

- 60 g Tinned green lentils
- 1 Garlic clove, finely diced
- 1 cm fresh ginger, finely diced
- 1 Bire's eye stew, finely crushed
- 150 g Celery cut into 2cm lengths
- 1 tsp Mild curry powder
- 130 g Tomato, cut into eight pieces
- 100 ml Chicken or vegetable stock
- 1 tbsp Chopped parsley

Instructions:

1.   Warm the stove

2.   Start with preparing the hot celery. Warm a skillet over medium-low warmth, including the olive oil, at that point the onion, garlic, ginger, stew, and celery. Fry tenderly for 2–3 minutes or until mellowed yet not shaded. At that point, include the curry powder and cook for a further moment.

3.   Add the tomatoes, then the stock and lentils, and stew delicately for 10 minutes. You might need to increment or reduction the cooking time contingent upon how crunchy you like your celery.

4.   Meanwhile, blend the turmeric, oil, and lemon squeeze and rub over the salmon. Place on a heating plate and cook for ten minutes.

5.   To complete, mix the parsley through the celery and present it with the salmon.

6.   Your dish is ready to serve.

36)   Shrimp Coronation Salad

Serving: 1

Nutritional Value: 105 calories

Preparation time: 5 minutes

Cook time: 0 minutes

Total time: 5 minutes

Ingredients:

- 75 g Natural yogurt
- One Bird's eye stew
- 1/2 tsp Mild curry powder
- 100 g Cooked shrimps
- Juice of 1/4 of a lemon
- One tsp Coriander, finely chopped
- One tsp ground turmeric
- 20 g Red onion, diced
- Walnut parts, finely diced
- 40 g Rocket, to serve
- One Medjool date, finely diced

Instructions:

1.   Blend the yogurt, lemon juice, coriander, and flavors together in a bowl.

2.   Include all the rest of the things and serve on a bed of the arugula leaves.

3.   Eat well and stay healthy and fresh.

37)   Spicy Chickpea Stew with Baked Potatoes

Serving: 4

Nutritional Value: 358 calories

Preparation time: 10 minutes

Cook time: 1 hour

Total time: 1 hour and 10 minutes

Ingredients:

*   Two red onions, finely cleaved

*   4-6 heating potatoes, pricked everywhere

*   2 x 400g tins cleaved tomatoes

*   2cm ginger, ground

*   Two tablespoons olive oil

*   cloves garlic, ground or squashed

*   ½ - 2 teaspoons bean stew chips (contingent upon how hot you like things)

*   Two yellow peppers (or whatever shading you prefer), cleaved into bite-size pieces

*   Two tablespoons turmeric

*   Two tablespoons cumin seeds

*   Sprinkle of water

*   Two tablespoons unsweetened cocoa powder (or cacao)

- 2 x 400g tins chickpeas

- Two tablespoons parsley in addition to extra for embellish

- A side plate of mixed greens, discretionary

- Salt and pepper to taste, discretionary

Instructions:

1. Preheat the stove to 200C. In the interim, you can set up the entirety of your mixings.

2. When the broiler is hot enough, placed your heating potatoes in the stove and cook for 1 hour or until they are done how you like them.

3. Once the potatoes are in the stove, place the olive oil and slashed red onion in an enormous wide pan and cook tenderly, with the cover on for five minutes, until the onions are delicate yet not earthy colored.

4. Remove the cover and include the garlic, ginger, cumin, and bean stew. Cook for a further moment on a low, warm stove, at that point, include the turmeric and an exceptionally little sprinkle of water and cook for one more moment, taking consideration not to let the dish get excessively dry.

5. Next, include the tomatoes, cocoa powder, chickpeas (counting the chickpea water), and yellow pepper. Bring to a bubble, at that point, stew on low warmth for 45 minutes until the sauce is thick and unctuous. The stew ought to be done at generally a similar time as the potatoes.

6. Finally, mix in the two tablespoons of parsley and some salt and pepper in the event that you wish it to be spicy, and serve the stew on the prepared potatoes, maybe with a basic side plate of mixed greens.

7. Enjoy your meal.

38)   Kale and Red Onion Dhal with Buckwheat

Serving: 4

Nutritional Value: 420 calories

Preparation time: 5 minutes

Cook time: 25 minutes

Total time: 30 minutes

Ingredients:

- One tablespoon olive oil
- One little red onion, cut
- 160g buckwheat (or earthy colored rice)
- 400ml coconut milk
- Two garlic cloves, ground or squashed
- Two cm ginger, ground
- 200ml water
- One birds-eye bean stew, deseeded and finely diced (more if you like things hot)
- Two teaspoons turmeric
- Two teaspoons garam masala
- 160g red lentils
- 100g kale (or spinach would be an extraordinary other option)

Instructions:

1.   Put the olive oil in an enormous, profound pan and include the cut onion. Cook on a low warmth, with the top on for five minutes until mellowed.

2.   Add the garlic, ginger and bean stew and cook for 1 minute.

3.   Add the turmeric, garam masala, and a sprinkle of water and cook for one minute.

4.   Add the red lentils, coconut milk, and 200ml water.

5.   Mix everything together completely and cook for 20 minutes over a delicately heat with the cover on. Mix once in a while and include somewhat more water if the dhal begins to stick.

6.   After 20 minutes, including the kale, mix all together and supplant the top, cook for a further 5 minutes.

7.   About 15 minutes before the curry is prepared, place the buckwheat in a medium pan, and include a lot of bubbling water. Take the water back to the bubble and cook for ten minutes. Channel the buckwheat in a strainer and present with the dhal.

8.   Your dish is ready to be served.

39)   Choc Chip Granola

Serving: 8

Nutritional Value: 244 calories

Preparation time: 10 minutes

Cook time: 20 minutes

Total time: 30 minutes

Ingredients:

- 200g normal sized oats
- 50g walnuts, generally cleaved
- Two tbsp light olive oil
- 20g margarine
- One tbsp brown colored sugar
- Two tbsp rice malt syrup
- 60g dim chocolate chips

Instructions:

1.   Preheat the broiler to 160°C. Line a huge heating plate with a silicone sheet or preparing material.

2.   Combine the oats and walnuts in an enormous bowl. In a little non-stick container, delicately heat the olive oil, spread, earthy colored sugar, and rice malt syrup until the margarine has liquefied and the sugar and syrup have broken down.

3.   Try not to permit to bubble. Pour the syrup over the oats and mix completely until the oats are completely secured.

4.   Distribute the granola over the heating plate, spreading directly into the corners.

5.   Leave clusters of blend with separating instead of an even spread. Prepare in the stove for 20 minutes until just touched brilliant earthy colored at the edges.

6.   Remove from the broiler and leave to cool on the plate totally.

7.   When cool, separate the greater knots on the plate with your fingers and afterward blend in the chocolate chips.

8.   Scoop or empty the granola into an impenetrable tub or container.

9.   The granola will save for fourteen days so you can make it in bulk.

40)   Parmesan Chicken and Kale

Serving: 4

Nutritional Value: 402 calories

Preparation time: 10 minutes

Cook time: 19 minutes

Total time: 29 minutes

Ingredients:

•   Two tablespoons olive oil

•   1/2 pound scampi

•   Fit salt

•   Newly ground dark pepper

•   One medium yellow onion, diced

•   Two cloves garlic, minced

•   Squeeze red pepper drops

•   One enormous bundle level leaf kale (around 12 ounces), stems evacuated and leaves coarsely cut

•   1/2 cup dry white wine

•   1/2 cup ground Parmesan cheddar

•   One tablespoon newly made lemon juice

Instructions:

1.   Warm the oil in a huge skillet keep the stove on medium heat until sparkling. Include the scampi into it, season with salt and pepper, and sauté until cooked thoroughly for five to seven minutes. Move the scampi to a plate and spread it with some wrap to keep warm.

2.   Include the onion, garlic, and pepper pieces to the skillet. Sauté until the onions are beginning to mollify, around two minutes. Mix in the kale, wine, and a touch of salt. Spread and cook for around five minutes, mixing every so often, until the kale is simply delicate.

3.   Add the scampi and any amassed juices to the skillet. Include the Parmesan and lemon squeeze and mix it thoroughly. Taste and season with increasingly salt and pepper according to your liking.

4.   It is ready to be served.

41)   Caesar Salad

Preparation Time: 12 minutes

Cooking Time: 12 minutes

Serving: 4

Ingredients:

• Garlic pepper, one tsp.

• Garlic minced and mashed, one clove

• Romaine lettuce, chopped

• Fresh shredded Asiago cheese

• Toasted croutons.

• Hellman's mayonnaise, half cup

- Finely grated parmesan cheese, half cup
- Buttermilk, 1/4 cup
- Sweet and sour dressing, half cup
- Dry Ranch dressing mix, two tsp.

Instructions:

1. Combine the ingredients for the dressing.

2. Add dressing to the lettuce, to taste.

3. Mix well and refrigerate.

4. Serve topped with shredded Asiago cheese and toasted croutons.

42) Caribbean Salad with Grilled Prawns

Preparation time: 10 minutes

Cooking Time: 10 minutes

Serving: 2

Ingredients:

- Teriyaki Sauce, half cup
- Tortilla chips
- Iceberg lettuce, half cup
- Pineapple chunks, half cup
- Cabbage, half cup
- Olive oil, half cup
- Jalapeno peppers three tbsp.

- Onion, diced, half cup
- Cilantro, two bunches
- Tomatoes, half cup
- Honey, two tbsp.
- Sugar, one tsp.
- Sesame oil, one tsp.
- Lime juice, one tsp.
- Wine vinegar, one and a half tsp.
- Grilled prawns
- Apple cider vinegar, one tbsp.

Instructions:

1. Marinate the chicken in the teriyaki for at least two hours.

2. Use a plastic bag. Put in fridge.

3. Preheat outdoor or indoor grill.

4. Grill the prawns for 4-5 mins.

5. Toss the lettuces and cabbage together and divide into 2 large serving size salad bowls.

6. Divide the pineapple and sprinkle on salads.

7. Break tortilla chips into large chunks and sprinkle on salads.

8. Slice the grilled prawns and divide among bowls.

9. Pour the dressing into two small bowls and serve with the salads.

43)   Caribbean Salad with Shrimps

Preparation time: 10 minutes

Cooking Time: 10 minutes

Serving: 2

Ingredients:

- Teriyaki Sauce, half cup
- Tortilla chips
- Iceberg lettuce, half cup
- Pineapple chunks, half cup
- Cabbage, half cup
- Olive oil, half cup
- Jalapeno peppers three tbsp.
- Onion, diced, half cup
- Cilantro, two bunches
- Tomatoes, half cup
- Honey, two tbsp.
- Sugar, one tsp.
- Sesame oil, one tsp.
- Lime juice, one tsp.
- Wine vinegar, one and a half tsp.
- Shrimps
- Apple cider vinegar, one tbsp.

Instructions:

1. Marinate the shrimps in the teriyaki for at least two hours.

2. Use a plastic bag. Put in fridge.

3. Preheat outdoor or indoor grill.

4. Grill the shrimps for 4-5 mins.

5. Toss the lettuces and cabbage together and divide into 2 large serving size salad bowls.

6. Divide the pineapple and sprinkle on salads.

7. Break tortilla chips into large chunks and sprinkle on salads.

8. Place the grilled shrimps and divide among bowls.

9. Pour the dressing into two small bowls and serve with the salads.

44) Spicy Shrimp Tacos

Preparation time: 10 minutes

Cooking Time: 10 minutes

Serving: 3

Ingredients:

- Tortilla, three
- Shrimps, six
- Iceberg lettuce, half cup
- Cabbage, half cup
- Avocado, two slices
- Chili powder, a pinch

- Mayonnaise, three tbsp.
- Onion, diced, half cup
- Thai sweet chili sauce, one tbsp.
- Siracha, one tbsp.

Instructions:

1. Heat a grill pan over medium heat and wipe surface with olive oil.

2. Season the shrimp with the salt, pepper and chili powder, and then grill for three to five minutes until done.

3. In a small bowl, mix together the mayo, sweet chili sauce and siracha together.

4. Warm the tortillas and place half of the cabbage on each tortilla.

5. Drizzle half the sauce over each taco.

6. Top with shrimp & garnish with avocado.

7. Serve immediately.

45)   Zuppa Toscana Soup

Preparation time: 10 minutes

Cooking Time: 35 minutes

Serving: 4

Ingredients:
- Water, two cups
- Minced garlic, one tbsp.
- Butter, four tbsp.

- Heavy cream, two cups
- Chopped kale, two cups
- Onion, half
- Ground fish sausage, half pound
- Salt and pepper to taste
- Potatoes, half cup

Instructions:
1. Mix all the ingredients together in a large pot.
2. Cook for 35 minutes and then serve hot.

46) Herb Grilled Salmon

Preparation time: 10 minutes
Cooking Time: 15 minutes
Serving: 4

Ingredients:
- Salmon fillet, two pounds
- Lemon, two, cut in halves
- Butter, half cup
- Italian seasoning, two tbsp.
- Steamed rice, two cups
- Parsley, half cup
- Minced garlic, one tsp.
- Salt and pepper to taste

Instructions:

1.   Season the salmon with salt, pepper, and Italian Seasoning, rubbing them well on both sides.

2.   Allow the salmon to briefly marinade on a slotted tray, at least for fifteen minutes.

3.   Place the salmon on the grill skin side down and brush with oil on both sides. You may also use cooking spray.

4.   Cook the salmon, flipping it regularly until it is cooked through.

5.   Bring your butter out from the chiller & slice a half cm thick ring. Return any excess back to the chiller, and discard any paper wrapping of the cut portion.

6.   Once the salmon is cooked, serve it with rice, lemon wedges, your garlic butter on top, and your choice of vegetables.

47)   Chicken Scampi

Preparation time: 10 minutes

Cooking Time: 20 minutes

Serving: 4

Ingredients:

- Olive oil, two tbsp.

- Minced garlic, one and a half tsp.

- Flour, one tbsp.

- Heavy cream, two cups
- Onion, half cup
- Scampi, half pound
- Salt and pepper to taste
- Parmesan cheese, half cup
- Mix bell peppers, sliced
- Angel hair, twelve ounces

Instructions:

1. Season scampi.

2. Place flour in a shallow dish and season with one tsp seasoned salt.

3. Dredge scampi in flour.

4. Heat one tbsp. olive oil in large skillet.

5. Place scampi in skillet and cook over medium high heat for four minutes. Flip and cook for three to four more minutes. Remove to a plate.

6. Add one tbsp. oil to skillet.

7. Add peppers and onions. Season with salt and pepper. Sauté for about five minutes.

8. Add garlic and sauté for a few more minutes.

9. Add cream, milk, and parmesan. Bring to a simmer.

10. Add scampi and let simmer for five minutes.

11. Your dish is ready to be served.

48)   Shrimp Alfredo

Preparation time: 10 minutes

Cooking Time: 20 minutes

Serving: 4

Ingredients:
- Olive oil, two tbsp.
- Minced garlic, one and a half tsp.
- Flour, one tbsp.
- Butter, four tbsp.
- Heavy cream, two cups
- Parsley, half cup
- Shrimp, half pound
- Salt and pepper to taste
- Parmesan cheese, half cup
- Pasta, one cup

Instructions:

1.   Add oil into a pan and then garlic.

2.   Add butter, cream and flour and mix until uniform mixture is formed.

3.   Add shrimps and cook and then add pasta.

4.   Serve in a bowl with parsley and parmesan cheese on top.

49)   Hickory Bourbon Salmon

Preparation time: 20 minutes

Cooking Time: 20 minutes

Serving: 3

Ingredients:

- Bourbon, one cup
- Soy sauce, two tbsp.
- Chopped chives, one tsp.
- Brown sugar, two tbsp.
- Salt and pepper to taste
- Salmon fillet, one pound
- Olive oil, two tbsp.
- Garlic powder, half tsp.

Instructions:

1.   Combine pineapple juice, brown sugar, bourbon, soy sauce, pepper and garlic powder in a bowl.

2.   Stir to dissolve sugar. Add the oil.

3.   Remove skin and bones from salmon fillets.

4.   Put fillets in baking dish and pour marinade over and let sit in the fridge for one hour or longer.

5.   The longer it can sit the more the marinade seeps into the fillets.

6.   Cook the salmon filets on the grill or on the stove top on medium heat.

7.   Brush the extra marinade over the fillets as they are cooking.

8.   Arrange the fillets on a plate and sprinkle with the chopped chives.

50)   New Orleans

Preparation time: 10 minutes

Cooking Time: 15 minutes

Serving: 4

Ingredients:
- Tilapa fillet, two pounds
- Shrimp, one pound
- Butter, four tbsp.
- Creole seasoning, two tbsp.
- Alfredo sauce, half cup
- Olive oil, three tbsp.
- Minced garlic, one tsp.
- Salt and pepper to taste

Instructions:

1.   Preheat oven to 425 degree.

2.   Wash and dry tilapia fillets, spread with olive oil and creole seasoning, to your taste.

3.   Place in well oiled baking pan, bake for ten minutes, until just white.

4.   While fish is baking, warm Alfredo in a small saucepan.

5.   In a fry pan, melt three tbsp. butter, add minced garlic and cleaned, prepared shrimp sauté for about five minutes.

6.   When fish is ready, remove pan from oven.

7.   Carefully remove fillets to plates, top with cooked shrimp and Alfredo sauce.

4.3 Dinner Recipes

51)   Kale, Edamame and Tofu Curry

Serving: 4

Nutritional Value: 342 calories

Preparation time: 10 minutes

Cook time: 35 minutes

Total time: 45 minutes

Ingredients:

- 200g kale leaves stalks evacuated and torn
- One tbsp rapeseed oil
- Two cloves garlic stripped and ground
- One red bean stew, deseeded and meagerly cut
- One enormous onion, diced
- One enormous thumb size (7cm) ginger, removed and ground
- 1/2 tsp ground turmeric
- One tsp paprika

- 1/2 tsp ground cumin
- 1/4 tsp cayenne pepper
- 1 tsp salt
- 250g dried red lentils
- 50g solidified soy edamame beans
- 200g firm tofu slashed into solid shapes
- One liter bubbling water
- Two tomatoes, generally slashed
- Juice of 1 lime

Instructions:

1.   Put the oil in an overwhelming bottomed container over a low-medium stove. Include the onion and cook for 5 minutes before including the garlic, ginger and bean stew and cooking for a further 2 minutes. Include the turmeric, cayenne, paprika, cumin, and salt. Mix thoroughly before including the red lentils and mixing once more.

2.   Pour in the bubbling water and make a generous stew by boiling for ten minutes, at that point decrease the warmth of the stove and cook for a further 20-30 minutes until the curry has a thick consistency.

3.   Add the soya beans, tofu, and tomatoes and cook for a further five minutes. Include the lime juice and kale leaves and cook until the kale is simply delicate.

4.   Your dish is ready to be served.

52) Grilled Salmon

Preparation time: 10 minutes

Cooking Time: 15 minutes

Serving: 4

Ingredients:

- Salmon fillet, two pounds
- Butter, half cup
- Italian seasoning, two tbsp.
- Steamed rice, two cups
- Parsley, half cup
- Minced garlic, one tsp.
- Salt and pepper to taste

Instructions:

1.   Season the salmon with salt, pepper, and Italian seasoning, rubbing them well on both sides.

2.   Allow the salmon to briefly marinade on a slotted tray, at least for fifteen minutes.

3.   Place the salmon on the grill skin side down and brush with oil on both sides. You may also use cooking spray.

4.   Cook the salmon, flipping it regularly until it is cooked through.

5.   Bring your butter out from the chiller & slice a half cm thick ring.

6.   Once the salmon is cooked, serve it with rice, your garlic butter on top, and your choice of vegetables.

53)   Parmesan Shrimp Pasta

Preparation time: 10 minutes

Cooking Time: 20 minutes

Serving: 4

Ingredients:

- Olive oil, two tbsp.
- Minced garlic, one and a half tsp.
- Flour, one tbsp.
- Butter, four tbsp.
- Heavy cream, two cups
- Parsley, half cup
- Shrimp, half pound
- Salt and pepper to taste
- Parmesan cheese, half cup
- Pasta, one cup

Instructions:

1.   Add oil into a pan and then garlic.

2.   Add butter, cream and flour and mix until uniform mixture is formed.

3.   Add shrimps and cook and then add pasta.

4.   Serve in a bowl with parsley and parmesan cheese on top.

54)   Ranch Pasta

Preparation time: 10 minutes

Cooking Time: 20 minutes

Serving: 2

Ingredients:

*   Olive oil, two tbsp.
*   Mayonnaise, one tbsp.
*   Frozen peas, four tbsp.
*   Buttermilk, one cup
*   Ranch dressing, half cup
*   Salt and pepper to taste
*   Ricotta cheese, half cup
*   Pasta, one cup

Instructions:

1.   Bring a pot of water to a boil and cook pasta.

2.   Drain into a colander and rinse with cold water until pasta is cool.

3.   Set pasta aside and allow to dry for about thirty minutes.

4.   While pasta is cooking, combine mayonnaise, buttermilk, ranch dressing mix, and season salt in a large bowl and mix until combined.

5.   Add in frozen peas and stir. The peas will thaw a bit during mixing and will finish thawing while pasta cools.

6.   Add dry rotini and mix until well blended.

7.   Your pasta is ready to be served.

55)   Miso Marinated Cod with Stir-Fried Greens:

Serving: 1

Nutritional Value: 450 calories

Preparation time: 12 minutes

Cook time: 20 minutes

Total time: 22 minutes

Ingredients:
- 50g kale, generally cut
- One garlic clove, finely diced
- One tbsp mirin
- 200g skinless cod filet
- One tbsp additional virgin olive oil
- 20g miso 60g green beans
- 40g celery, cut
- 20g red onion, cut
- One tsp finely crushed new ginger

- One tsp ground turmeric
- One tsp sesame seeds
- 5g parsley, usually cut
- 30g buckwheat
- One tbsp tamari

Instructions:

1.   Warm the stove to 220°C.

2.   Blend the miso, mirin, and one teaspoon of the oil. Rub everywhere throughout the cod and leave to marinate for 30 minutes. Prepare the cod for 10 minutes.

3.   In the interim, heat a huge griddle or wok with the rest of the oil. Include the onion and sautéed food for a couple of moments. At that point include the celery, garlic, stew, ginger, green beans, and kale. Hurl and fry until the kale is delicate and cooked through. You may need to add a little water to the skillet to help the cooking procedure.

4.   Cook the buckwheat as indicated by the parcel guidelines with the turmeric for 3 minutes.

5.   Include the sesame seeds, parsley, and tamari to the sautéed food and present with the greens and fish.

6.   Your dish is ready to be served.

56)   Potato Soup

Preparation time: 12 minutes

Cooking Time: 30 minutes

Serving: 6

Ingredients:

- Cornstarch, two tbsp.
- Potato, two
- Green Onions, chopped, three
- Ginger, grated, half tsp.
- Water, two tbsp.
- Chicken broth, four cups
- Soy Sauce, one tbsp.

Instructions:

1.   Mix all the ingredients together, and boil it for about thirty minutes.

2.   Add the cornstarch in the end, and mix properly.

3.   Your soup is ready to be served.

57)   Toowoomba Pasta Recipe

Preparation Time: 20 minutes

Cooking Time: 30 minutes

Serving: 4

Ingredients:

- Parmesan cheese, half cup
- Fettuccini, one box
- Cornstarch, one tbsp.
- Garlic powder
- Ketchup, two tbsp.
- Olive oil, one tbsp.
- Cream, one tbsp.
- Shrimps, half pound
- Small onion, diced, one
- Butter, two tbsp.
- Large mushrooms, sliced, four
- Salt and pepper, to taste

Instructions:

1. Cook fettuccine as directed.
2. Melt butter in a large skillet.
3. Whisk in cream, ketchup and spices.
4. Bring to a boil.

5.	Continue to simmer and reduce while you continue with the rest of the recipe, stirring occasionally with a wire whisk.

6.	Sauté mushrooms in a separate small skillet over medium to low heat, in olive oil until soft.

7.	Add mushrooms to simmering sauce.

8.	Cook shrimp in the small skillet in olive oil just until pink and add to sauce.

9.	Simmer for about five minutes adding green onions for the last two minutes or so.

10.	In a large bowl, toss shrimp mixture with cooked and drained fettuccine and serve immediately, topping with finely shredded fresh parmesan cheese.

11.	Your dish is ready.

58)	Seafood Stuffed Mushrooms

Preparation time: 10 minutes

Cooking Time: 25 minutes

Serving: 6

Ingredients:
•	Oil, one quart
•	Garlic powder, half tsp.
•	Eggs, two
•	Milk, one cup
•	Crab meat, half pound

- Wheat flour, half cup
- Fresh mushrooms, one pound
- Cheddar cheese, half cup
- Salt, half tsp.
- Oyster crackers, two cups
- Red bell peppers, two
- Onions, one
- Celery, a quarter cup

Instructions:

1. Preheat oven to 400 degrees.

2. Wash mushrooms and remove stems.

3. Set caps aside, and chop half of the stems.

4. Sauté chopped mushroom stems, celery, onion and pepper in butter for two minutes.

5. Transfer to a plate and cool in refrigerator.

6. Combine sautéed vegetables and all other ingredients and mix well.

7. Place mushroom caps in a sprayed or buttered baking pan stem side up.

8. Spoon one tsp stuffing into each mushroom cap.

9. Cover with a piece of sliced cheese.

10. Bake for fifteen minutes until cheese is lightly brown.

59)   Lobster Bisque

Preparation time: 10 minutes

Cooking Time: 30 minutes

Serving: 4

Ingredients:

- Water, six cups
- Fish stock, two cups
- Green Onions, chopped, three
- Carrot, one cup
- Celery, one cup
- Lobsters, one pound
- Ginger, grated, half tsp.
- White wine, two tbsp.
- Potato, two
- Cream, one cup
- Cognac, a quarter cup
- Tomatoes, one and a half cup
- Paprika and thyme, one tbsp.
- All-purpose flour, one cup

Instructions:

1.   Place the water, the white wine and the fish stock into a wide, deep pot, and bring to a boil on high heat.

2.   Place lobsters, topside down, in the broth.

3.   Reduce heat to medium and cook covered for approximately six minutes.

4.   Remove lobsters from broth and put them to the side.

5.   When the lobsters are cool enough to handle, begin removing the meat from the shell, dicing the pieces into half inch cubes.

6.   Store the lobster meat in the refrigerator until later.

7.   Place the lobster shells back into the broth, reduce heat to a simmer and cook uncovered for twenty minutes.

8.   Strain the broth through a sieve into a container and store in the refrigerator until later.

9.   Discard the lobster shells.

10.   Put your pot back on the stove under medium heat.

11.   Pour in the melted butter.

12.   Once the butter is heated up, add the onions, carrots, celery and garlic.

13.   Add the cognac and cook until the alcohol has evaporated.

14.   Mix in the flour, stirring with a heavy gauge spatula or spoon until the mixture is blond in color and has a buttery aroma.

15.   Mix the diced tomatoes, paprika, thyme and ground pepper with the cold broth from the refrigerator.

16.   Then, pour the broth slowly into the butter and vegetable mixture.

17.   Cook uncovered for thirty minutes under medium low heat, stirring frequently so not to burn.

18.   Remove bisque from heat.

19.   Blend small amounts of bisque in blender and then puree.

20.   Puree all of the bisque and pour pureed bisque back into pot with remaining amount.

21.   Add chopped lobster meat and heavy cream, heat and serve.

22.   If the soup is too thick, thin it by adding milk or water prior to serving.

23.   Your dish is ready to be served.

60)   Super Salmon Salad:

Serving: 1

Nutritional Value: 98 calories

Preparation time: 15 minutes

Cook time: 0 minutes

Total time: 15 minutes

Ingredients:

*   80g avocado, stripped, stoned and cut

*   40g celery, cut

*   50g chicory leaves

*   100g smoked salmon cuts

*   One huge Medjool date, hollowed and cut

*   20g red onion, cut

*   15g pecans cut

*   One tbsp extra-virgin olive oil

*   Juice ¼ lemons

- 10g parsley finely cut
- One tbsp capers
- 10g lovage or celery leaves, cut
- 50g arugula leaves

Instructions:

1.   Mix the serving of mixed greens leaves on an enormous plate.

2.   Combine all the rest of the things and serve on the leaves.

3.   Your salad is ready to be served.

61)   Baked Salmon with Mint Dressing:

Serving: 1

Nutritional Value: 340 calories

Preparation time: 10 minutes

Cook time: 10 minutes

Total time: 20 minutes

Ingredients:
- One little bunch (10g) parsley, generally cut
- One salmon filet (130g)
- 40g spinach leaves
- radishes, cut and meagrely cut
- 40g blended serving of mixed greens leaves

- 5cm piece (50g) cucumber, cut into lumps
- Two spring onions, cut

For the dressing:

- Salt and newly ground dark pepper
- 1 tsp low-fat mayonnaise
- 1 tbsp rice vinegar
- 1 tbsp regular yogurt
- Two leaves mint, finely diced

Instructions:

1. Preheat the broiler to 200°C.

2. Place the salmon filet on a heating plate and prepare for 16–18 minutes until simply cooked through. Remove from the broiler and put it in a safe spot. The salmon is similarly decent hot or cold in the plate of mixed greens.

3. If your salmon has skin, basically cook skin side down and expel the salmon from the skin utilizing a fish cut in the wake of cooking. It should slide off effectively when cooked.

4. In a little bowl, combine the mayonnaise, yogurt, rice wine vinegar, mint leaves, and salt and pepper together and leave for 5 minutes to permit the flavors to create.

5. Arrange the plate of mixed greens leaves and spinach on a serving plate and top with the radishes, cucumber, spring onions, and parsley. Piece the cooked salmon onto the serving of mixed greens and sprinkle the dressing over.

6. Your salad is ready to be served.

62) Green Salad Skewers:

Serving: 2

Nutritional Value: 306 calories

Preparation time: 30 minutes

Cook time: 10 minutes

Total time: 40 minutes

Ingredients:

- huge dark olives
- wooden sticks, let it absorb water for 30 minutes before use
- 100g feta, cut into eight 3D squares
- ½ red onion cut down the middle and isolated into eight pieces
- cherry tomatoes
- One yellow pepper, cut into eight squares
- 100g cucumber, cut into four cuts and split

For the dressing:

- 1 tsp balsamic vinegar
- 1 tbsp additional virgin olive oil
- ½ clove garlic, stripped and squashed
- Juice of ½ lemon
- Liberal flavoring of salt and newly ground dark pepper
- Not many leaves basil, finely slashed
- ½ tsp dried blended herbs to supplant basil and oregano

Instructions:

1.   Thread each stick with the plate of mixed greens things: olive, tomato, yellow pepper, red onion, cucumber, feta, tomato, and olive, yellow pepper, red onion, cucumber.

2.   Place all the dressing ingredients in a little bowl and combine completely. Pour over the sticks.

3.   Your dish is ready to be served.

63)   Buckwheat Pasta Salad

Serving: 1

Nutritional Value: 112 calories

Preparation time: 10 minutes

Cook time: 0 minutes

Total time: 10 minutes

Ingredients:

•   Two cherry tomatoes halved

•   A huge bunch of rocket

•   A little bunch of basil leaves

•   1/2 avocado, diced

•   20g pine nuts

•   Two olives

•   50g buckwheat pasta (cooked as per the bundle instructions)

•   One tbsp. additional virgin olive oil

Instructions:

1.   Tenderly consolidate all the above mentioned ingredients with the exception of the pine nuts and decorate on a plate or in a bowl

2.   Dissipate the pine nuts over the top.

3.   Your salad is ready to be served.

64)   Garlic Shrimp Skewers

Preparation time: 10 minutes

Cooking Time: 30 minutes

Serving: 4

Ingredients:

•   Worcestershire sauce, one tsp.

•   Shrimp, two pound

•   Minced garlic, half tsp.

•   Butter, two tbsp.

•   Lemon juice, half cup

•   Wooden skewers

•   Salt and Pepper to taste

Instructions:

1.   In a medium saucepan melt the butter over medium heat.

2.   Add the garlic and sauté for a couple of minutes.

3.   Remove from heat.

4.   Add lemon juice, Worcestershire sauce, garlic powder, salt, and pepper.

5.   Allow the sauce to cool.

6.   Reserve half of the sauce in a bowl for brushing.

7.   Mix the renaming half of the sauce with the raw shrimp and marinate for thirty minutes.

8.   Thread the shrimp onto the wooden skewers.

9.   Heat an outdoor grill to medium-high heat.

10.   Place the shrimp skewers onto the grill and cook while brushing with the reserved marinade for a few minutes per side or until the shrimp are pink.

11.   Your dish is ready to be served.

65)   Shrimp Popcorn

Preparation time: 10 minutes

Cooking Time: 10 minutes

Serving: 4

Ingredients:
- Shrimp, two pound
- Minced garlic, half tsp.
- Milk, two tbsp.
- All- purpose flour, one cup
- Egg, one

- Oil, half cup
- Seasoned salt, one tsp.
- Salt and Pepper to taste

Instructions:

1. Preheat oil to 350 degrees.

2. Combine half cup oil and egg; beat well.

3. Add remaining ingredients except oil for frying and stir until well blended.

4. Dip shrimp into batter to coat.

5. Drop shrimp into hot oil and fry for a few minutes or until golden brown.

6. Remove with slotted spoon; drain on paper towel.

7. Your dish is ready to be served.

66) Nashville Hot Shrimp

Preparation time: 10 minutes

Cooking Time: 10 minutes

Serving: 4

Ingredients:
- Shrimp, two pound
- Minced garlic, half tsp.
- Milk, two tbsp.
- All- purpose flour, one cup

- Egg, one
- Nashville pepper, three tbsp.
- Oil, half cup
- Seasoned salt, one tsp.
- Salt and Pepper to taste

Instructions:

1. Preheat oil to 350 degrees.

2. Combine half cup oil and egg; beat well.

3. Add remaining ingredients except oil for frying and stir until well blended.

4. Dip shrimp into batter to coat.

5. Drop shrimp into hot oil and fry for a few minutes or until golden brown.

6. Remove with slotted spoon; drain on paper towel.

7. Your dish is ready to be served.

67) Shrimp Linguini Alfredo

Preparation time: 10 minutes

Cooking Time: 20 minutes

Serving: 4

Ingredients:

- Olive oil, two tbsp.
- Minced garlic, one and a half tsp.

- Flour, one tbsp.
- Butter, four tbsp.
- Heavy cream, two cups
- Parsley, half cup
- Shrimp, half pound
- Salt and pepper to taste
- Parmesan cheese, half cup
- Linguini pasta, one cup

Instructions:

1.   Add oil into a pan and then garlic.

2.   Add butter, cream and flour and mix until uniform mixture is formed.

3.   Add shrimps and cook and then add the linguini pasta.

4.   Serve in a bowl with parsley and parmesan cheese on top.

68)   Crab Linguini Pasta

Preparation time: 10 minutes

Cooking Time: 20 minutes

Serving: 4

Ingredients:

- Olive oil, two tbsp.
- Minced garlic, one and a half tsp.

- Flour, one tbsp.
- Butter, four tbsp.
- Heavy cream, two cups
- Parsley, half cup
- Crab meat, half pound
- Salt and pepper to taste
- Parmesan cheese, half cup
- Linguini pasta, one cup

Instructions:

1. Add oil into a pan and then garlic.

2. Add butter, cream and flour and mix until uniform mixture is formed.

3. Add crab meat and cook and then add the linguini pasta.

4. Serve in a bowl with parsley and parmesan cheese on top.

69) Vegetarian Pizza

Preparation time: 10 minutes

Cooking Time: 30 minutes

Serving: 8

Ingredients:

- Pizza dough, one box

- Garlic powder, half tsp.

- Mushrooms, one cup

- Chili powder, one tsp.

- Olive oil, one tsp.

- Mozzarella cheese, shredded, one cup

- Mixed vegetables, one cup

- Olives, half cup

Instructions:

1.   Heat oil in large skillet.

2.   Add vegetables and cook, stirring frequently until lightly soft.

3.   Stir in seasonings into the mixture.

4.   Heat oven to 425 degrees.

5.   Sprinkle pizza pan with semolina flour and press dough into pan.

6.   Pre-bake dough until it is a very light golden brown, about six minutes.

7.   Remove from oven and scatter vegetables, mushrooms, olives on the crust, and top with cheese.

8.   Bake for another fifteen minutes until crust is golden brown.

9.   Your pizza is ready to be served.

70)   Macaroni Salad

Preparation time: 10 minutes

Cooking Time: 10 minutes

Serving: 1

Ingredients:

- Boiled macaroni, as required
- Ketchup, half cup
- Salt and Pepper
- Mayonnaise, half cup
- Powdered sugar, one tbsp.
- Whole milk, a quarter cup
- Sweetened condensed milk, half cup
- Cheddar cheese cubes, one cup
- Pineapple chunks, half cup
- Capsicum, half cup
- Sweet corn, half cup
- Cabbage, half cup

Instructions:

1.   Measure all the ingredients in a large salad bowl and mix really well.

2.   Chill in fridge for a couple hours before serving.

3.   Your dish is ready.

71)   Crunchy Thai Salad

Preparation time: 10 minutes

Cooking Time: 10 minutes

Serving: 4

Ingredients:

- Chopped cilantro, 1/4 cup
- Chili Lime Vinaigrette, one tbsp.
- Sweet and Spicy Peanut Sauce, one tbsp.
- Shredded red cabbage, one cup
- Medium carrots peeled and shredded, two
- Shelled edamame, half cup
- Sliced almonds toasted, half cup
- Wonton Strips
- Napa or Savory cabbage chopped, half cup
- Fresh spinach coarsely chopped, two cups
- Green onions thinly sliced, three

For Frying the Shrimps:

- Butter, half tsp.
- Olive oil, two tbsp.
- Chili powder, half tsp.
- Cayenne pepper, half tsp.
- Minced garlic, one tsp.
- Raw shrimp peeled and deveined, eight ounces

Instructions:

1.   In a large self-sealing plastic bag, combine shrimp, minced garlic, chili powder, and cayenne.

2.   Toss until shrimps are evenly coated with the spice mix.

3.   Heat a large, heavy skillet over medium high heat. Melt olive oil and butter and swirl to coat the bottom of the skillet.

4.   Add shrimps in a single layer. Pan-fry for about 2 minutes, then turn and fry until shrimps become pink all the way through and slightly firm, about 2-3 minutes. Do not overcook the shrimps.

5.   Carefully remove from skillet and set aside.

6.   Assemble the salad.

7.   Layer or toss cabbages, spinach, carrots, edamame, green onions, and sliced almonds, wonton strips, and cilantro in bowl.

8.   Serve with Chili-Lime Vinaigrette and Sweet & Spicy Peanut Sauce.

9.   Garnish with additional cilantro and wonton strips.

72)   Double Crunch Shrimp

Preparation Time: 10 minutes

Cooking Time: 10 minutes

Serving: 2-3

Ingredients:

For Sauce:

•   Chili bean paste, two tbsp.

•   Chili paste, one tsp.

•   Cornstarch, one tsp.

- Chicken broth, half cup
- Oyster sauce, two tbsp.
- Sherry, half cup

For Shrimps:

- Salt and pepper, to taste
- Seasoning salt, to taste
- Oil, for cooking
- Water, two tbsp.
- Panko, one cup
- Flour, one cup
- Shrimp, one and a half pounds
- Eggs, two

Instructions:

1. Use the shrimps by cutting vertically down the back of the shrimp. Leave tails on.

2. Season shrimp with salt, pepper, and seasoning salt.

3. Heat enough oil to deep fry the shrimp in a skillet to 350 degrees.

4. Put panko crumbs in a shallow dish. Add seasonings to taste and mix well.

5. Put flour in a separate shallow dish.

6. Beat the eggs and water together.

7. Dip the shrimps in the egg-water mixture.

8. Add the shrimps to the flour.

9. Dip again in egg-water mixture.

10.   Toss shrimps in panko crumbs.

11.   Fry in hot oil at 350 degrees F until golden, about 3 minutes.

12.   Drain the fried shrimps on the cooling racks over paper towels.

13.   In a large pot mix together all of the ingredients for the sauce, making sure that the cornstarch dissolves thoroughly.

14.   Heat a wok or large skillet on high heat with a teaspoon of oil.

15.   Add the sauce and let it simmer for 1 minute to thicken. Add the shrimps, toss to coat, and simmer for 1 more minute.

16.   Your crunchy shrimps are ready to serve.

73)   California Roll

Preparation Time: 15 minutes

Cooking Time: 30 minutes

Serving: 4

Ingredients:
- Rice vinegar, quarter cup
- Granulated sugar, two tbsp.
- Salt, half tsp.
- White rice, two cups
- Water, two cups

For Sriracha Mayo Crab:

- Light mayonnaise, a quarter cup

- Sriracha, two tbsp.

- Crab meat, twelve ounces

For Toppings:

- Julienned carrots

- Large avocado

- English cucumber, (thinly sliced)

Instructions:

1.   Add the rice to a fine mesh strainer, and run under cold water for 1-2 minutes, rinsing until the water runs clear.

2.   Allow the rice to thoroughly drain, and then transfer it to a medium saucepan with two cups of water.

3.   Place on high heat and bring the rice to a boil.

4.   Once boiling, reduce the heat to low, and cover with a lid. Simmer 15 minutes. Remove from heat and allow to rest, undisturbed, and covered, for 15 additional minutes.

5.   While you wait, place a small nonstick pan over medium heat.

6.   Add the rice vinegar, sugar, and salt. Cook, stirring with a whisk, until the sugar has dissolved completely.

7.   Remove from the burner to allow to cool down slightly.

8.   When the rice is ready, pour the vinegar mixture over the top of the rice, and stir to thoroughly mix.

9.   Fold until all of the vinegar mixture has been absorbed by the rice.

10.   To a small mixing bowl, combine the crab meat with the sriracha, and mayonnaise. Mix well.

11.   In four bowls add the rice and layer with crab mixture, cucumber slices, carrots, diced avocado, sesame seeds, and micro greens.

12.   Drizzle with soy sauce, and serve right away.

74)   Dragon Roll

Preparation time: 15 minutes

Cooking Time: 60 minutes

Serving: 4

Ingredients:

- Lemon, half
- Nori sheets, two
- Sushi rice, two cups
- Shrimp tempura, eight pieces
- Tobiko, two tbsp.
- Unagi (eel)
- Persian/Japanese cucumbers, one
- Avocados, one

Instructions:

1.   Gather all the ingredients.

2.   Cut cucumber lengthwise into quarters.

3.   Remove the seeds, and then cut in half lengthwise.

4.   Cut the avocado in half lengthwise around the seed, and twist the two halves until they separate.

5.   Hack the knife edge into the pit. Hold the skin of the avocado with the other hand, and twist in counter directions.

6.   Remove the skin, and slice the avocado widthwise.

7.   Gently presses the avocados slices with your fingers, and then keep pressing gently, and evenly with the side of the knife until the length of avocado is about the length of sushi roll.

8.   Wrap the bamboo mat with plastic wrap, and place half of the nori sheet, shiny side down.

9.   Turn it over and put the shrimp tempura, cucumber strips, and tobiko at the bottom end of the nori sheet.

10.   If you like to put unagi, place it inside here as well.

11.   From the bottom end, start rolling nori sheet over the filling tightly, and firmly with bamboo mat until the bottom end reaches the nori sheet.

12.   Place the bamboo mat over the roll and tightly squeeze the roll.

13.   Using the side of the knife, place the avocado on top of the roll.

14.   Place plastic wrap over the roll and then put the bamboo mat over.

15.   Cut the roll into 8 pieces with the knife.

16.   Put tobiko on each piece of sushi, and drizzle spicy mayo, and sprinkle black sesame seeds on top.

17.   Your dish is ready to be served.

75)   Cobb Salad

Preparation Time: 10 minutes

Total Time: 10 minutes

Serving: 4

Ingredients:

- Cucumber, peeled and cubed, half cup
- Cherry tomatoes, cut in half
- Garbanzo beans, rinsed, one cup
- Cooked quinoa, a quarter cup
- Slivered almonds, three tbsp.
- Sunflower seeds to sprinkle on top
- Cracked pepper
- Romaine Lettuce, two
- Asparagus spears, cut, four grilled
- Green beans, cut, half cup
- Cubed roasted golden beets, half cup
- Avocado, cubed, half

Instructions:

1. Place cut Romaine lettuce on plate.

2. Place all cut vegetables in sections on the salad greens.

3. Mix the quinoa with the slivered almonds and place quinoa in the middle of the salad.

4. Drizzle your preferred dressing on top and serve.

4.4 Recipes for Juices, Sweet Dishes and Snacks

76)   Muesli

Ingredients:

*   100g strawberries, hulled and diced

*   10g buckwheat puffs

*   15g coconut drops or dried up coconut

*   20g buckwheat cereal

*   40g Medjool dates, hollowed and diced

*   10g cocoa nibs

*   15g pecans, diced

*   100g plain Greek yogurt (or vegetarian type, for example, soya or coconut yogurt)

Instructions:

1.   Blend the entire of the above things together.

2.   Possibly including the yogurt and strawberries before serving before making it in mass.

3.   Your dish is ready to be served.

77)   Banana Blueberry Pancakes with Apple Compote and Turmeric Latte

Serving: 2

Nutritional Value: 105 calories

Preparation time: 13 minutes

Cook time: 10 minutes

Total time: 23 minutes

Ingredients:

For preparing the Pancakes

- 225g blueberries
- Six bananas
- 150g oats
- Six eggs
- Two tsp baking powder
- ¼ teaspoon salt

For preparing the Apple Compote

- 1/4 teaspoon cinnamon powder
- Two apples
- One tablespoon lemon juice
- Five dates (pitted)
- salt to taste

For preparing the Turmeric Latte

- stripped ginger root
- One teaspoon turmeric powder
- Touch of dark pepper (expands ingestion)
- One teaspoon cinnamon powder
- Three cups of coconut milk
- One teaspoon crude nectar
- Touch of cayenne pepper (discretionary)

Instructions:

1.   Put the oats in a rapid blender and let it grind for one moment or until an oat flour has framed. You should ensure that your blender is dry before doing this, or probably everything will get spongy.

2.   Presently include the bananas, eggs, heating powder and salt to the blender and grind for 2 minutes until a smooth mixture structures.

3.   Move the blend to an enormous bowl and overlay in the blueberries. Leave to rest for 10 mins while the baking powder actuates.

4.   To make your cakes, include a bit of margarine to your skillet on a medium-high stove. Include a couple of spoons of the blueberry cake blend and fry for until pleasantly brilliant on the base side. Hurl the flapjack to sear the opposite side.

5.   Remove the center and flat cleave your apples.

6.   Pop everything in a food processor, along with two tablespoons of water and a touch of salt. Grind it to shape your stout apple compote.

7.   Mix all the things in a rapid blender until smooth.

8.   Fill it in a little container and warm for 4 minutes over a medium stove until hot yet not bubbling.

9.   Your pancakes are ready to be served along with your latte.

78)   Fish and Chips

Preparation Time: 10 minutes

Cooking Time: 10 minutes

Serving: 2-4

Ingredients:

- Large russet potatoes, peeled and cut lengthwise, four

- All-purpose flour, two cups

- Seafood seasoning, two tsp.

- Kosher salt, according to taste

- Peanut or vegetable oil, for frying

- Baking soda, one tsp.

- Cold beer, one bottle

- Haddock fillets, skinned and cut diagonally, two pounds

Instructions:

1. Warm the oil in a large pot over medium stove.

2. Heat the oil to 325 degrees.

3. Control the temperature with a treats thermometer.

4. Keep the potato sticks in a bowl of water to maintain the color of the potatoes before cooking.

5. Fry the potatoes until they are cooked through and delicate yet have no shading, around four to five minutes.

6. Delicately move the spoon around as the fries are cooking. Take them off from the oil and put them promptly on a paper towel lined heating sheet.

7. Preheat the stove to 300 degrees and raise the temperature of the cooking oil to 375 degrees.

8. In a medium bowl, mix the flour, seasoning, and touch of salt.

9.   At the point when the oil is preheated to the right temperature.

10.   Coat the fish liberally.

11.   While adding the fish to the oil, plunge half of the filet into the oil and permit the blender to begin puffing, and afterward delicately slide it into the oil.

12.   Fry the fish until they are brilliantly earthy colored and firm, around 5 minutes turning the fish over, during the cooking time.

13.   Move the fish to a serving platter, and present with the fries.

79)   Green Juice

Ingredients:
•   One medium pear, cut into eighths
•   stems of celery
•   One medium green apple, cut into eighths
•   1/2 huge cucumber, cut into quarters

Instructions:

1.   Squeeze all the things adhering to the directions for ordinary squeezing in your juicer manual.

2.   Drink quickly, or let chill for an hour and enjoy later.

80)   Chocolate and Coffee Mousse

Serving: 8

Nutritional Value: 242 calories

Preparation time: 4 hours

Cook time: 15 minutes

Total time: 4 hours and 15 minutes

Ingredients:

- Cinnamon 1/2 tsp 300 ml of Almond milk
- Cocoa powder 2 tbsp.
- Espresso 200 ml
- Gelatin powder 1 tbsp.
- Coconut yogurt 300 g
- Maple syrup 2 tbsp.
- Chocolate unadulterated 200 g

Instructions:

1.   Join the almond milk and espresso in a pan and sprinkle the gelatin over it. Let it be for 5 minutes.

2.   Mix the blend well and bring to bubble quickly. At that point, quickly remove the container from the stove.

3.   Mix the maple syrup, cinnamon, and the dim chocolate into the hot fluid. Keep on blending until the chocolate has totally dissolved and has been assimilated into the blend.

4.   Pour it in enriching pastry glasses and let it set in the refrigerator for approximately 4 hours.

5.   Prior to serving, decorate with a spoon of coconut yogurt and residue with cocoa.

6.   Your dish is ready to be served.

81)   Melon and Grape Juice

Serving: 2

Nutritional Value: 125 calories

Preparation time: 2 minutes

Cook time: 0 minutes

Total time: 2 minutes

Ingredients:

- 100g melon, stripped, deseeded and cut into pieces
- ½ cucumber, stripped however liked, split, seeds evacuated and diced
- 100g red seedless grapes
- 30g small spinach leaves, stalk less

Instructions:

1.   Blend together all the things in a blender and pour it out in glasses.

2.   Serve your juice right away.

82)   Black Current and Kale Smoothie

Serving: 2

Nutritional Value: 186 calories

Preparation time: 4 minutes

Cook time: 0 minutes

Total time: 4 minutes

Ingredients:

- One banana
- One tsp nectar
- One cup newly made green tea
- Five ice 3D shapes
- kale leaves, stalk less
- 40 g blackcurrants, washed

Instructions:

1. Mix the nectar into the warm green tea until properly mixed.

2. Prodigy all the things together in a blender until smooth.

3. Serve right away.

83) Green Tea Smoothie

Serving: 2

Nutritional Value: 183 calories

Preparation time: 3 minutes

Cook time: 0 minutes

Total time: 3 minutes

Ingredients:

- Two tsp matcha green tea powder
- Two bananas
- 250 ml of milk
- Three tsp nectar
- 1/2 tsp vanilla bean
- Five ice 3D squares

Instructions:

1. Basically, mix all the things together in a blender and serve in two glasses.

2. Drink it without storing it for later.

84)   Black current and Raspberry Jelly

Serving: 2

Nutritional Value: 76 calories

Preparation time: 2 minutes

Cook time: 15 minutes

Total time: 17 minutes

Ingredients:

- Two tbsp. granulated sugar
- 100g raspberries washed
- 100g blackcurrants washed
- 300ml water

- Two packs gelatin

Instructions:

1. Arrange the raspberries in two serving dishes/glasses/molds. Put the gelatin in a bowl of cold water to mollify.

2. Place the blackcurrants in a little skillet with the sugar and 100ml water and bring to bubble. Stew enthusiastically for 5 minutes and afterward remove it from the heat. Leave it in the open for 2 minutes.

3. Squeeze out abundant water from the gelatin leaves and add them to the pan. Mix until completely mixed, at that point mix in the remainder of the water. Empty the fluid into the readied dishes and refrigerate to set. These ought to be prepared in around 3-4 hours or overnight.

4. Your jelly after setting is ready to be served.

85) Chocolate Bites:

Ingredients:
- 250g Medjool dates pitted
- 30g dull chocolate broken into pieces; or cocoa nibs
- 1 tbsp cocoa powder
- 120g pecans
- 1 tbsp ground turmeric
- 1 tbsp additional virgin olive oil
- 1-2 tbsp water
- 1 tsp vanilla concentrate

Instructions:

1. Put the pecans and chocolate in a food processor and keep it processing until you have a fine powder.

2. Include the various things with the exception of the water and mix until the blend shapes a ball. You could conceivably need to include the water depending on the consistency of the blend. You don't need it to be excessively clingy.

3. Utilizing your hands, structure the blend into scaled-down balls, and refrigerate in a hermetically sealed compartment for approximately one hour before eating them.

4. You could move a portion of the balls in some more cocoa or dried up a coconut to accomplish an alternate completion if you like.

5. They can be stored up for a week.

6. Your dish is ready to be served.

7. Enjoy your meal.

86) Banana and Chocolate Smoothie

Preparation time: 5 minutes

Serving: 1

Ingredients:

• Frozen banana chunks, ½ cup

• Frozen chocolate chunks, ½ cup

• Peanut Butter ice cream, one scoop

- Low fat milk, one cup

Instructions:

1. Add all the ingredients in a blender and blend appropriately for three to four minutes.

2. Now pour into a cup and enjoy.

3. You can store this smoothie by freezing it.

4. Prior to using it later, you can re-blend the smoothie.

87) Mango and Pineapple Smoothie

Preparation time: 5 minutes

Serving: 1

Ingredients:
- Frozen mango chunks, ½ cup
- Frozen Pineapple chunks, ½ cup
- Vanilla ice cream, one scoop
- Low fat milk, one cup

Instructions:

1. Add all the ingredients in a blender and blend appropriately for three to four minutes.

2. Now pour into a cup and enjoy.

3. You can store this smoothie by freezing it.

4. Prior to using it later, you can re-blend the smoothie.

88) Superfood Smoothie

Preparation time: 5 minutes

Serving: 1

Ingredients:

- Frozen kiwi chunks, ½ cup
- Fresh spinach, ½ cup
- Cucumber chunks, ¼ cup
- Chia seeds, one tsp.
- Low fat almond milk, one cup
- Vanilla protein powder, ½ cup

Instructions:

1.   Add all the ingredients in a blender and blend appropriately for three to four minutes.

2.   Now pour into a cup and enjoy.

3.   You can store this smoothie by freezing it.

4.   Prior to using it later, you can re-blend the smoothie.

89) Greek Yoghurt and Berry Smoothie

Preparation time: 5 minutes

Serving: 1

Ingredients:

- Frozen berries chunks, ½ cup
- Frozen Greek yoghurt, ½ cup
- Peanut Butter ice cream, one scoop
- Low fat almond milk, one cup
- Vanilla protein powder, ½ cup

Instructions:

1. Add all the ingredients in a blender and blend appropriately for three to four minutes.

2. Now pour into a cup and enjoy.

3. You can store this smoothie by freezing it.

4. Prior to using it later, you can re-blend the smoothie.

90) Apple Pie Smoothie

Preparation time: 5 minutes

Serving: 1

Ingredients:

- Frozen apple chunks, peeled, ½ cup
- Vanilla extract, one tsp.
- Cinnamon powder, ¼ tsp.
- Nutmeg powder, ¼ tsp.
- Low fat milk, one cup

Instructions:

1.   Add all the ingredients in a blender and blend appropriately for three to four minutes.

2.   Now pour into a cup and enjoy.

3.   You can store this smoothie by freezing it.

4.   Prior to using it later, you can re-blend the smoothie.

91)   Red Berries Smoothie

Preparation time: 5 minutes

Serving: 1

Ingredients:

• Frozen red berries chunks, ½ cup

• Vanilla protein powder, ½ cup

• Low fat milk, one cup

Instructions:

1.   Add all the ingredients in a blender and blend appropriately for three to four minutes.

2.   Now pour into a cup and enjoy.

3.   You can store this smoothie by freezing it.

4.   Prior to using it later, you can re-blend the smoothie.

92)   Pear and Banana Protein Smoothie

Preparation time: 5 minutes

Serving: 1

Ingredients:

- Frozen banana chunks, ½ cup
- Vanilla protein powder, ½ cup
- Low fat milk, one cup
- Frozen Pear chunks, ½ cup

Instructions:

1.   Add all the ingredients in a blender and blend appropriately for three to four minutes.

2.   Now pour into a cup and enjoy.

3.   You can store this smoothie by freezing it.

4.   Prior to using it later, you can re-blend the smoothie.

93)   Tomato Smoothie

Preparation time: 5 minutes

Serving: 1

Ingredients:

- Lemon juice, two tbsp.
- Carrot juice, ½ cup

- Tomato juice, one cup
- Tomatoes peeled, ½ cup
- Celery Stalk chopped, one

Instructions:

1.   Add all the ingredients in a blender and blend appropriately for three to four minutes.

2.   Now pour into a cup and enjoy.

3.   You can store this smoothie by freezing it.

4.   Prior to using it later, you can re-blend the smoothie.

94)   Red Velvet Cake

Preparation Time: 15 minutes

Cooking Time: 35 minutes

Serving: 12

Ingredients:

- Cocoa powder, two cups
- Buttermilk, one cup
- Large eggs, two
- Food color, red
- All-purpose flour, two cups
- Salt, one tsp.
- Vanilla essence, one tsp.
- Vinegar, one tbsp.

- Baking soda, one tsp.
- Shortening, half cup
- Sugar, one and a half cup
- Butter, half cup

Instructions:

1. Cream butter and sugar; add eggs and blend.

2. Add food coloring, water, and cocoa.

3. Blend in buttermilk; add flour and salt gradually.

4. Add vanilla and beat until mixed. Mix vinegar and soda and stir in last; do not beat.

5. Pour into two nine- inch pans.

6. Bake for 30 to 35 minutes in a 350 degree oven. Frost with fluff frosting.

7. Add milk mixture and vanilla; continue beating.

8. When icing is very fluffy, frost cool cake.

95) Double Chocolate Smoothie

Preparation time: 5 minutes

Serving: 1

Ingredients:

- Frozen Greek Yoghurt, ½ cup
- Unsweetened Cocoa powder, ¼ tsp.

- Banana chunks, ¼ tsp.
- Chocolate protein powder, ¼ cup
- Low fat milk, one cup

Instructions:

1.   Add all the ingredients in a blender and blend appropriately for three to four minutes.

2.   Now pour into a cup and enjoy.

3.   You can store this smoothie by freezing it.

4.   Prior to using it later, you can re-blend the smoothie.

96)   Stout Irish Cream Cake

Preparation Time: 15 minutes

Cooking Time: 45 minutes

Serving: 12

Ingredients:

- Irish cream Liqueur, half cup
- Cream cheese, eight ounce
- Sugar, five cups
- Butter, one cup
- Stuat beer, one cup
- Sour cream, one cup
- Eggs, two
- All-purpose flour, one cup

- Vanilla essence, one tsp.

- Cocoa powder, half cup

Instructions:

1. Mix all the ingredients together and bake for 40 minutes approximately.

2. Dust sugar on top and serve.

97) Pumpkin Spice Smoothie

Preparation time: 5 minutes

Serving: 1

Ingredients:

- Frozen pumpkin puree, ½ cup

- Cinnamon powder, ¼ tsp.

- Ground ginger powder, ¼ tsp.

- Ground cloves powder, ¼ tsp.

- Decaffeinated Coffee, ¾ cup

- Vanilla protein powder, 1/4cup

- Low fat milk, one cup

Instructions:

1. Add all the ingredients in a blender and blend appropriately for three to four minutes.

2. Now pour into a cup and enjoy.

3.   You can store this smoothie by freezing it.

4.   Prior to using it later, you can re-blend the smoothie.

98)   Artichoke and Spinach Dip

Preparation time: 5 minutes

Cooking Time: 35 minutes

Serving: 10

Ingredients:

- Cream cheese, eight ounces

- Artichoke, ten ounces

- Garlic Alfredo sauce, sixteen ounces

- Chopped spinach, ten ounces

- Mozzarella cheese, shredded, two cups

- Parmesan and cheddar cheese mix, shredded, one cup

Instructions:

1.   Mix all ingredients in a large bowl.

2.   Pour into crock pot and set on high for 35 minutes.

3.   Your dip is ready to serve.

99)   Original Cheesecake

Preparation Time: 10 minutes

Cooking Time: 10 minutes

Serving: 5

Ingredients:

- Sour cream, half cup
- Large eggs, five
- Vanilla extract, two tsp.
- Graham crackers, one and a half cup
- Ground Cinnamon, half tsp.
- Butter, half cup
- Sugar, one and a half cup

Instructions:

1. Use an electric mixer to mix cream cheese, sugar, sour cream and vanilla and cinnamon.

2. Blend until smooth and creamy.

3. Scrape down sides of bowl.

4. Whisk eggs in a bowl; add to cream cheese mixture. Blend just until eggs are incorporated.

5. Add the graham cracker layer which is made by combining butter and graham crackers together first and then the cream cheese mixture.

6. Freeze the mixture for one hour and serve with sour cream on top.

100) Chocolate Frosties

Preparation Time: 5 minutes

Cooking Time: 10 minutes

Serving: 4

Ingredients:

- Milk, one cup
- Vanilla ice-cream, four scoops
- Chocolate milk powder, eight tbsp.

Instructions:

1. Allow the ice cream to soften just enough to blend easily

2. Mix everything thoroughly in a blender.

3. Once everything is thoroughly combined, mix until you have reached the desired softness.

4. Serve right away in glasses, with spoons.

All the recipes mentioned in this chapter are easy to make by yourself at home.

Conclusion

Our daily life revolves around our busy schedules. In this routine, finding something healthy to eat becomes less of a priority especially for individuals that work vigorously to earn for their families. In such conditions, health is compromised to a greater extent that can cause many side effects in the future. To avoid such conditions it is very important to not only eat healthy but also to eat right.

This book covers the life of a Pescatarian, making it easy for them to prepare their favorite recipes inside their kitchen without any stress. This book explains how a Pescatarian diet differs from other diets and how it can be beneficial to a human being who wants to lose weight while eating healthy food.

Being a Pescatarian is no more boring or difficult with all these amazing breakfast, lunch, dinner, snacks, juices, and sweets recipes mentioned in this book. You will also get a seven day diet plan that you can change according to your taste and preferences with the variety of recipes mentioned in the book. So, there is no need to wait more when you can cook healthy and yummy right in your home.

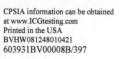

CPSIA information can be obtained
at www.ICGtesting.com
Printed in the USA
BVHW081248010421
603931BV00008B/397